Seeking Christ:
Colossians for Women

By
Lauren Bassford

ISBN-10: 1-58427-538-3

ISBN-13: 978-1-58427-538-1

All graphics and photos from istockphoto.com

Cover design by Joanna Clem; Layout by Kyle Pope

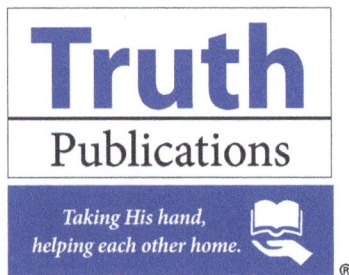

Truth
Publications

*Taking His hand,
helping each other home.* ®

Truth Publications, Inc.
CEI Bookstore
220 S. Marion St., Athens, AL 35611
855-492-6657
sales@truthpublications.com
www.truthbooks.com

Table of Contents

Introduction

Introduction

Colossians is a book that gets overlooked sometimes. Its content is pretty similar to Ephesians, and it's shorter, so we turn to Ephesians to get a fuller view of basically the same points. Yet, Colossians is unique in several ways. In particular, Paul spends more time in Colossians talking about the glory of Jesus and the effect that glory has on the redemptive work that He accomplished on the cross. This puts the application points in a different light, and a different context, than we find them in Ephesians. It also gives us a different logical understanding of the reasoning behind the applications Paul makes.

This study, then, will look at Colossians as a whole. We'll look at the rich doctrinal understanding of Jesus that Paul lays out in the beginning of the book, even though that usually gets passed over. Frankly, this often gets passed over because it can be intimidating. The structure of Paul's writing lends itself to long sentences in English and complex phrases and clauses. It's easy to look at the descriptions of Jesus's glory and work and decide that just making a list of application points will be sufficient.

Without a good understanding of the doctrine underneath, though, the instructions of the rest of the book are hollow and difficult to achieve. Once we get a handle on Paul's argument about how we should understand Jesus and what He's done for us, we'll be able to understand the familiar application points of Colossians in their proper context—one that puts everything we do in relation to the preeminence of Jesus.

Paul's Prayers
Colossians 1:1-12

Lesson 1: Paul's Prayers

Paul starts off Colossians with a bang. Even his self-introduction is rich with meaning and import. Paul starts off by introducing himself as an apostle of Jesus, by the will of God. He lets his readers know right at the outset that He belongs to Jesus. He is an apostle of Jesus—no more, no less. And this apostleship isn't his own decision, or his own work. He quickly acknowledges that it's God's will that he is where and what he is. We don't really see the detailed defense of his apostleship that we get in other letters, but Paul is still quick to make sure his readers understand why he's writing and what his qualifications are to write and instruct them. Timothy is named as a co-author, and is just listed as "our brother." While Paul is quick to remind the Colossians that he's teaching from God and by God's will, he's also quick to remind them that they are all brothers—Paul, Timothy, and the little old widow lady at the church in Colossae are all equal as heirs in Christ.

Paul then offers a greeting, which he frequently does in his letters. However, even his greeting is on message and teaches important truths. He greets them with grace and peace. "Grace" was a traditional greeting among Greeks of the day, and "peace", *shalom*, remains a traditional

greeting among Jews to this day. Even in this seemingly simple greeting, Paul begins his message. How easy would it have been for Paul, a Jew, to offer a greeting of peace to his audience and move on? Paul is a Jew! Peace is how Jews greet one another. Paul would just be speaking the language of his people. Or, alternatively, if Paul knows he is speaking to a Gentile audience, he could attempt to speak to them in the language they understand. He could abandon his own identity to reach out to his audience. Paul might tell himself, "they understand 'grace' as a greeting, so 'grace' is what I'll use."

Instead, Paul offers both. Both, together! And with that he begins one of the primary messages of the book—one of the primary messages of his ministry, that Jews and Gentiles are one in Christ. Not that either abandons the entirety of their identity, but that the two combine to make something better, something more whole, with the work of Jesus joining the two. That's why it's significant that Paul offers a greeting of grace and peace in God. Not grace and peace as the world offers or as the world defines them, but as God the Father of all of us gives us when we allow Him to work in us.

Paul then turns to his prayer for the Colossians. In this passage, he's more describing his prayers as opposed to actually praying in the text of the letter. He begins with thankfulness. What an incredible reminder for us! Rather than asking God for things on their behalf, or using his prayer to remind the Colossians of their trespasses, he begins the prayer by thanking God for them. Specifically, he's thankful for their faith, their love for the saints, and the hope that they have. These ideas are all connected to one another. Their faith in God reinforces their love for one another and increases the hope that they have for their heavenly home. Their love increases their faith, as they see God's way working, and helps them look forward even more to the eternity that they hope for. Their hope gives definition to their faith and encourages them to keep actively loving each other. All of these work together. Of course, this isn't the only time we've seen these ideas linked together. Probably the most famous is in 1 Corinthians 13, where faith, hope, and love are the three that remain after spiritual gifts have ceased.

These three attributes—faith, love, and hope aren't something that the Colossians came up with on their own or that they are responsible for fostering within themselves. Paul says in 1:5 that they came from the word of truth, the gospel. With this, Paul starts in on another of his major themes for this book: the work of Jesus and the gospel in the Christian. We'll come back to this in more detail later, but it's important here that Paul says the faith, love, and hope that they have are a result of the work of the gospel in them.

This hearing of faith, love and hope through the gospel didn't just affect the brethren in Colossae. Paul says that this process happened all over the whole world. Nor was it a small, limited effect. He says that through the whole world, the gospel is bearing fruit and increasing, as it does in Colossae. The picture Paul draws, then, is one of a virtuous cycle. The gospel works faith, love, and hope in the Christian. As they tell others about the good news, faith, love, and hope grow in those new Christians, but also continue to grow in the original Christian who's

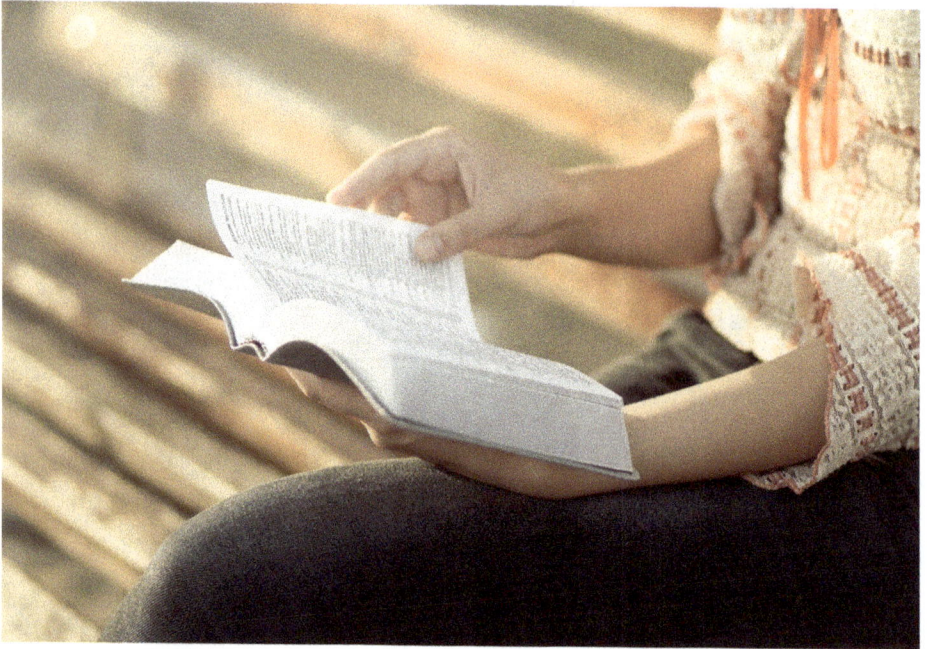

doing the spreading. The same process plays out today, of course. Is there anything that more affirms the faith, love, and hope that we have in Christ than seeing it take root in a new believer? God's plan for spreading His good news is a good plan!

Paul then takes a brief side trip to talk about Epaphras, the one with whom he credits the Colossians having heard the gospel. This seems a bit of a non-sequitur—here we are thanking God for the faith of the Colossians, and then we're name dropping? Two reasons present themselves for why Paul would interject this statement. First, Paul hasn't actually been to Colossae—this letter is something of a spiritual blind date for him. Part of what he's doing here is trying to connect with the Colossian brethren as he can, to remind them that he knows Epaphras well and that he and the Colossians are connected through Epaphras.

Additionally, though, he's been talking about the great work done through the gospel and is about to talk about that even more. He wants to make sure they remember the one who taught them. I think that's an important lesson for us, as well, as we consider those men who dedicate their lives and livelihood to teaching the gospel. It's easy to take the located preacher for granted *("Oh, that's just Epaphras, I teach his kids in Bible class, I sit behind his wife in ladies' class")* and forget about the awesome responsibility he's taken on! Preachers are glad to do it, but let's be sure to remember the ones who teach us about the gospel and to reward them for so doing! In this case, Epaphras's reward comes in the form of an "attaboy" from Paul, and an "attaboy" is always a good idea. Sometimes that reward will come in the form of special prayers, notes of thanks, encouraging comments about them, or even gifts. Those who teach us the gospel give us an immeasurably great gift. We should be sure to remember the debt we owe those who teach us!

The subject of Paul's prayers then changes from his thankfulness for the Colossians to the things he would ask of God on their behalf. Specifically, everything he would ask for them falls under the subject heading of knowledge and understanding. He asks that God will fill them with a knowledge of His will, and that they'll have spiritual wisdom and understanding. He wants them to get it! He wants them to really understand, at a gut level, all that God has done for them, and what God wants for them.

But then Paul gets heavy. In 1:10-11, he turns to the subject of walking worthy. We might think, "I'm already overwhelmed!" He wants them to walk worthy of the Lord, to be fully pleasing, to bear fruit, to increase in knowledge, to be strong in power, to have endurance and patience and joy. He even wants *(as he moves into 1:12)*, for them to be qualified to join in the inheritance. That is an incredibly overwhelming

To do list

list. At least for me, and for most women I know, this passage starts morphing into a *to-do list*. I've got to be worthy, fully pleasing, fruit bearing, knowledgeable, strong, enduring, patient, joyful, qualified. *"Phew. I can't. I give up,"* we might say to ourselves.

Our culture's answer to this conundrum is to remind us that we are enough. That's everywhere. You are enough. You're enough for your kids, just doing the best you can. Enough for your husband, your job, your housekeeping, whatever it is. The problem is, I don't feel like I'm enough. I know I'm not enough! If that list is what I need to accomplish, I am most definitely not enough!

The problem is with the focus. Paul goes on in 1:12 to encourage their thankfulness. He cites their giving thanks to the Father as another piece of their walking worthy and says that they ought to be giving thanks for His having qualified them to share in the inheritance. "Oh, wait," we ask, "I don't qualify myself? God qualifies me?" That puts the whole *to-do list* in an entirely different light. These are not attributes that I need to dredge up within myself and perfect by myself in order to prove myself worthy. Instead, these are the ways in which God qualifies me. As He works in me, I become pleasing, fruit-bearing, knowledgeable, strong, enduring, patient, joyful, qualified. I still have work to do, and Paul will go on at length about that later in the book. I am not the ultimate actor. God is at work in me, and that's what makes me worthy.

Thought Questions

1. What do we make of Paul and Timothy and their motivation for writing?

2. Where do faith, love, and hope show up in your life?

3. Have you seen the word of truth bearing fruit and increasing? What effects does it have?

4. Who taught you the gospel? Who teaches you now? Brainstorm how you can show your appreciation for the great gift you've been given!

5. Where are you in your journey to being filled with the knowledge of God's will? What's your next step?

6. Do you feel like you walk worthy? Why or why not?

7. What parts of the journey toward worthy walking are most intimidating to you? Do you believe that God can work in you to make you worthy in that area?

8. What are you most thankful for in your worthiness journey? What has God already done in your life that you can praise Him for?

Christ Jesus
Colossians 1:13-18

Lesson 2: Christ Jesus

From discussing his prayers for the Colossian brethren, Paul pivots very neatly into a discussion of Jesus. In our *verse-by-verse, search-for-meaning* way of reading the Bible, sometimes these pivots can seem to us like very abrupt subject changes. Discussion point one: Prayers. Discussion point two: Jesus. In reality, Paul ties all of it together. This isn't a subject change as much as a smooth transition. He has just talked about his prayers for them—what he is asking God to do on their behalf. It's natural, then, to turn to talking about Jesus, who is the instrument God uses to accomplish the things Paul prayed for!

This is also a reminder to the Colossians that God is active, working, and powerful. It can be easy to think of God as passive and disinterested. He made all this, got it going, and now is sitting back and watching. There are any number of good responses as to why that's not an accurate portrayal of the God of the Bible, but Paul sets out one of those responses here: God is active in your redemption and transference to the kingdom of His beloved Son! When Paul prays to Him, God is active on behalf of the Colossians, and similarly on our behalf as well.

Paul starts in, then, on a series of comparisons. In each of these, Jesus is the best of some category or type. In verse 15, Jesus is the best deity, and the firstborn of creation. In verse 16, He is over all authorities and the linchpin of creation. In verse 17, He is what holds creation together. Finally, in verse 18, He's the head of the body and the firstborn from the dead.

Overall, I think Paul has a couple of reasons for using so many comparisons. First, he's adopting what we'd call different learning styles today. If you're teaching a classroom of children, you don't just lecture at them. You lecture some, you have them read some, you write on the board some, you have them do some worksheets, and you may have them model or act out the concept in some way. Some kids will pick up on the ideas by hearing them. Some kids will learn best by reading. Some need to get up and be active in order to learn. By hitting all of the various learning styles, everyone will get the information somewhere. Similarly, in this text, Paul is communicating with people from various walks of life. A former Jew might not get Jesus as the very best of a variety of possible gods, but a former Gentile will. A midwife might understand anatomy language, like the head of the body, better than a marketplace trader would. A young person might not really appreciate Jesus as being over all authorities, but a governmental official would certainly grasp that.

Another reason, has to do with emphasis. Modern American culture usually turns up its nose at repetition. In anything other than kids' literature it's considered unnecessary and condescending. In worship culture it's often considered vain. In ancient cultures, though, repetition was used purposefully. In Revelation, for instance, when various groups cry out and call the Lord *"Holy, holy, holy,"* it's not just because they like the word and it rolls off the tongue. The repetition indicates emphasis, similar to our superlative forms. To call God *"Holy, holy, holy"* is to say that He is not just good, not just better, He's the very best! Paul is using a similar form here, where Jesus isn't just good at this or that, He's the best at everything, the best of the best.

Zeus

In 1:15, Jesus is the image of the invisible God. He is the best of all the gods the Colossians have experienced. They're very used to image-based representations of gods. While they might worship Zeus or Athena, they direct that worship toward an image of the god. The image makes the god

Athena

more accessible—while a noncorporeal god is difficult to comprehend, I can at least somewhat wrap my mind around the statue in front of me. Jesus is similar to those statues in that He gives His followers something comprehensible to represent the nature of their God to them. Unlike the statues of Zeus or Athena, though, Jesus is real. Statues of Zeus or Athena don't do anything to help anyone, don't move or reach out, and don't look at their followers with compassion or understanding. Jesus is a representation of the invisible God that actually interacts with His followers! Jesus is Immanuel—He's God, but He's with us!

Jesus is also the Firstborn of all creation in 1:15. This doesn't mean that Jesus is a created being. Instead, this description evokes the importance of the heir. In Psalm 89:27, the psalmist speaking for God calls David the firstborn. In a literal sense, David was not the firstborn. He was the youngest of eight, according to 1 Samuel 16. However, in the ancient world, being the firstborn sometimes had little to do with actual birth order. It's a pattern that we see multiple times in the Bible. *Firstborn* had more to do with the first right of inheritance than first in birth order. Jesus, then, is the heir of all creation. He is the Son who has inherited the power to run God's kingdom. He is, of course, also the Son that the wicked tenants killed in Matthew 21:33-46. As the firstborn inherits the promises, so Jesus inherited the promises first.

In 1:16-17, Paul describes Jesus's role as the Creator of everything, emphasizing His creation of all authorities. Paul then goes on a preposition spree—by Him, through Him, for Him, after Him *(He was before all things)*, in Him. Basically, Jesus was the creative force behind the creation of everything! Paul, however, makes a special point of calling Jesus the Creator of thrones, dominions, rulers and authorities. This is significant in a way that we might miss. Throughout the ancient world, and especially in Greek and Roman culture, the divine right of kings wasn't just a philosophical idea. The emperors, especially the Caesars, declared themselves gods. They ruled because they asserted divine powers for themselves. In calling Jesus the Creator of the rulers and authorities, Paul puts Jesus at the top of the heap of all governments demanding obedience. Not only is Jesus the image of the invisible God, the one who is better than other gods, He also made all those other authorities who consider themselves gods! Jesus is, therefore, the best of all possible governmental authorities, as well.

Jesus is also declared to be the head of the body in 1:18. 2,000 years removed from the writing of this letter, we reflexively finish the thought: "the head of the body, the church." To us, body = church in the Bible. And while it does, it's important for us to remember that the analogy was new to them at the writing of this letter, so they likely read it in a much more literal sense. The head is the director of the body; it tells the body where to go. The head also gives life to the body—if I'm still breathing, but I have no brain activity, the word for that is *braindead*. Without the head operating appropriately, the body isn't truly alive. The head is also part of the body, but still distinct from it. Jesus is the Director, the life source, a part but also separate from the church just as surely as the head is to the body.

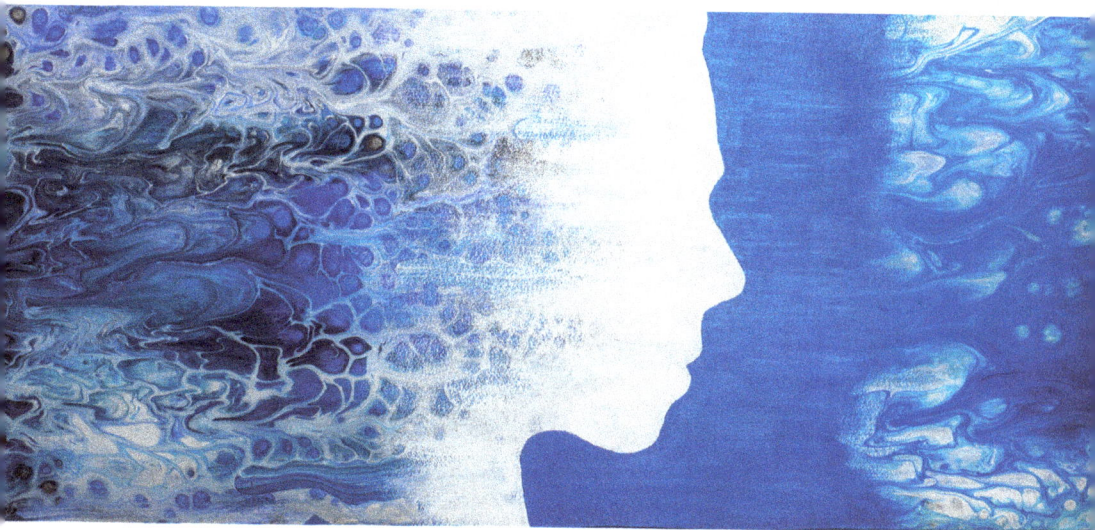

Finally, in 1:18, Paul says that Jesus is the beginning. Specifically, Jesus is the beginning by being the firstborn from the dead. This calls us back to our discussion of Jesus being the firstborn of all creation. Again, this doesn't mean that Jesus is a created being. In this case, it means that Jesus was the first to taste resurrection—at least, a particular type of resurrection. Lazarus was raised from the dead before Jesus, as was the widow's son from Nain and the daughter of Jairus. However, those three all died again and remain dead to this day. Jesus was the first to be raised from the dead and stay that way. That is so important for us because we hope for the same thing! Jesus is the beginning of God fulfilling the promise He made to all of His people that we would be raised to be with Him in eternity.

Thought Questions

1. Where have you seen God's work in your life to qualify you to walk worthy?

2. Which of the comparisons Paul makes speaks most clearly to you? Why?

3. How is Jesus the image of the invisible God in your life?

4. If Paul says Jesus is the firstborn of creation, how do we know that doesn't mean Jesus is a created being? Consider John 1:1-3; 8:58, and Psalm 89:27 in your answer.

5. If Jesus is the Creator of earthly governments, how does that inform our political involvement?

6. How much control and power does Jesus have over your local church body? How can you tell?

7. How important is Jesus in your daily walk? How can meditating on this section of Colossians help you make Him more central?

8. This lesson has been all about the surpassing greatness of Jesus. Praise Him! Pick one of the attributes Paul mentions in this section of Colossians and write praise for Jesus and His glory!

Reconciliation through Jesus Colossians 1:19-23

Lesson 3: Reconciliation through Jesus

Paul spent the last section of chapter one talking about how amazing Jesus is. He used analogy, word choice, and lots of variety to emphasize just how much better Jesus is than anything or anyone the Colossians had ever seen. In part, this was to help the Colossians understand why, when Paul prayed, He could fully expect that God would answer his prayers for the brethren in Colossae, and answer them fully. God is more powerful than we could possibly imagine! Just look at the representation of Him that we have in His Son, Jesus. Of course we can count on God to answer our prayers to deliver and qualify us, to make us worthy of the walk to which we've been called!

At the same time, though, talking about the greatness of Jesus is setting up Paul's discussion of the work that Jesus came to do—namely, the work of reconciling sinful people to a sinless God. This is really the linchpin of Paul's discussion of Jesus, and an important aspect for us to consider as well. Jesus didn't come just to give us an example or just to teach us how to live our best life. Jesus came to fix the biggest problem any of us have. We have all sinned, and because of that sin we have found ourselves alienated from God eternally. Jesus's work, then, was a turning point in the history of humankind, and we must always be careful not to dismiss its importance.

Paul begins this discussion by calling Jesus the dwelling place of God's fullness. It might be easy to read some of Paul's discussion of who Jesus is from the last lesson and come away thinking that Jesus is *big stuff* but still not all the way God—we might view Him as subordinate to God in some essential way. But Paul makes the point, that Jesus is entirely God. The fullness of God dwells within Jesus. Jesus is God, *full stop*. In fact, not only is Jesus the dwelling place of God's fullness, but the text says that God's fullness was pleased to dwell in Him. This is not your teenager helping out with the laundry, dragging feet, rolling eyes, and sighing loudly. God is pleased. This is right, the way it is supposed to be. Finally, the plan is in motion! While obviously it would have been preferable for mankind never to sin and never to need the mediation of a Savior, when Jesus came to earth, the plan that God had set in motion was coming to fruition in a real way. God is pleased to be able to take this next step in His plan and inhabit the body of Jesus.

The fullness of God wasn't just hanging out in Jesus, though. It dwelt with a purpose. The fullness of God dwelt in Jesus so that He could make peace. Jesus had an incredibly important job to do while He was on earth—to teach, yes, and demonstrate who He was, but most importantly, to make peace. Part of Paul's discussion here is showing the relevance of Jesus. Why are we so concerned in verses 13-18 with Jesus and His wonderfulness? Because He is wonderful, and He is God, but also because He is the instigator of the peace we can have with God. Without Jesus, there is no peace with God, there is no reconciliation.

And oh, how we need that reconciliation! Paul goes on to talk about exactly why the Colossians needed peace to be made between them and God. He begins verse 21 in the English Standard Version with the phrase, *"And you."* I hear a definite tone of voice in that *"And you,"* don't you? He does not have nice things to say about them. Of course, he's talking about them in the past tense, but still. He says that they were alienated. They were different, so different as to be almost unreachable. Alienated also has a pejorative sense about it—not just that they were different, but that they were different and less than they should be. They were also hostile in mind. Their minds weren't just different; they were hostile about it. They were opposed to God, but more than that, they took pleasure in being opposed to God. They regarded God as the enemy. Finally, they did evil deeds. They weren't just opposed to God in their minds. They were determined to show with their actions that they found God contemptible.

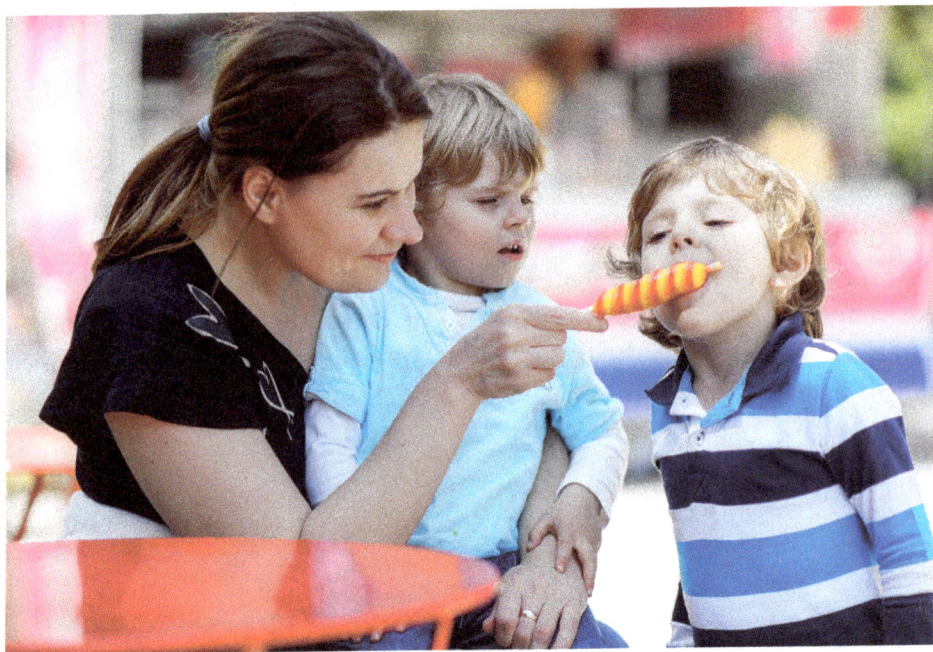

Sounds pretty awful, doesn't it? I mean, these people are just terrible! How could they be so horrible? Except, this is a description of anyone and everyone who is outside of Christ, anyone who needs His peacemaking work to bring them into fellowship with God. Sisters, I was alienated, hostile in mind, doing evil deeds. You were alienated, hostile in mind, doing evil deeds. The next door neighbor you have who's outside of Jesus, but who's a great neighbor, picks up your mail when you're out of town, and offers your kids popsicles when they're playing outside on hot days? Yep. Alienated, hostile in mind, doing evil deeds. This is not the picture of a serial killer—well, it is, but not just the serial killer. It's a picture of anyone at all who hasn't had Jesus work peace between them and God!

I think the application here is twofold. First of all, it's important for us to remember where we were. Especially if we were raised around God's people, it's easy to look at our previous lives and say, "Me? Not that bad! Jesus didn't have to work as hard for me as He did for So-and-So over there." There aren't different levels of alienation. If we're alienated, we're alienated! Also, though, we need to remember this when we look at our friends who need to hear about Jesus. Our friend doesn't just need to switch churches, and she'll be fine. If she's not in a relationship with Jesus that involves being baptized into Him for the forgiveness of her sins, then no matter how lovely a person she is, she too is alienated, hostile, and doing evil deeds!

Of course, that becomes even more pointed as Paul goes on in verse 22. Building on verse 21, Paul says that they were awful, awful, terrible people, and Jesus has taken them and reconciled them in His body of flesh by His death. Jesus didn't just reconcile them in His body, Paul specifies it was His body of flesh. It was a body that was like ours, that felt pain, that got tired, that got hungry. A body of flesh, in contrast to Jesus's spiritual existence before. A body of flesh, in contrast to God's fullness in its spiritual form. But it also wasn't just that Jesus reconciled them in His body of flesh. That body of flesh did the reconciling by His death.

While it's uncomfortable for us to consider, we need to think about the graphic nature of what was involved in this. Jesus, the dwelling place of the fullness of God, had a body that was like mine. In that body, He lived perfectly, never giving in to sin's temptations. Then, after living perfectly, He was taken by His own countrymen, beaten, and put to death in the most gruesome way they could come up with. He suffered like that for hours while being mocked by onlookers. He suffered, knowing His mother was standing right there, watching the whole thing. Then He died and was hurriedly taken off the cross and dealt with so that His murderers could be ritually clean for the Sabbath.

Now, pair that death, that path to reconciliation, with the description of the people He was reconciling. For the Colossians, and for me, who were alienated, hostile, evil deed-doers, the dwelling place of the fullness of God suffered and died in that fashion. Why? So that He could present me holy and blameless. He saw my shortcomings, and rather than saying, "Nope, who's next?" He saw what He could do to make me perfect and then went and did it.

This presentation of me, though, is not without condition. Paul makes it clear to the Colossians that there's an "if" attached to Jesus being willing to present them holy and blameless. Of course, that condition is entirely reasonable. They are made presentable before God if they continue. That's all He asks! They just need to continue—not attain perfection, just continuation in the faith that they've been taught. Paul will go into greater detail later in the book about just what that continuation looks like.

Thought Questions

1. What do we learn about Jesus's actions and death from Paul's description of Him as the dwelling place of God's fullness?

2. What kind of picture is painted of the person who is outside of Christ?

3. Think of someone you know who is outside of Jesus. Does your mental image of the person match up with this description?

4. What should change in the way in which we interact with our friends who need Jesus based on our understanding of Paul's description here?

5. What part of Jesus's reconciliation by His body of flesh in His death strikes you the most?

6. What should our reaction be to Jesus's sacrifice? Should we feel guilt, or something like Peter's reaction when Jesus washed the disciples feet—"Lord, you'll never!"? What reaction should we have?

7. Does the condition Jesus requires to present us "holy and blameless" seem reasonable to you? Why is it reasonable? Why might some consider it unreasonable?

8. Do you see any concepts at the end of this section that are repeated from earlier in the chapter? Make a list.

Paul's Struggles
Colossians 1:24-2:5

Lesson 4: Paul's Struggles

Paul has spent about half of chapter one talking about Jesus. He's talked at length about His excellence—He is the best of a whole series of categories. He's talked about Jesus's work in reconciling us and making peace. He's talked about Jesus's sacrifice; death in His body of flesh. Then, at the very end of chapter one, Paul turns to talking about himself and his struggles.

On a quick reading, this seems somewhat inappropriate. To go from talking about Jesus, the dwelling place of God's fullness, who sacrificed Himself on the cross, to talking about yourself might seem a little

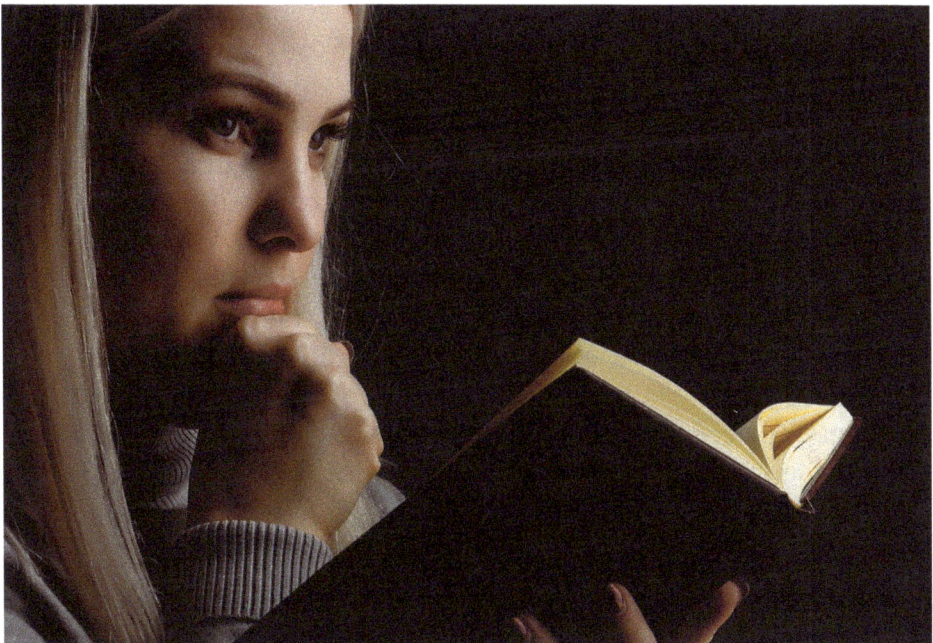

narcissistic. However, that's not what's going on here at all. Instead, Paul is explaining his *why.* Paul is about to talk about the various struggles he faces as a minister and servant of the gospel. Of course talking about that on the heels of contemplating his Savior makes sense! If Jesus wasn't so excellent, if He hadn't done His work, if He hadn't made His sacrifice, none of Paul's struggles would make any sense at all. Conversely, because of *who He is,* and *what He did,* Paul's struggles make complete sense.

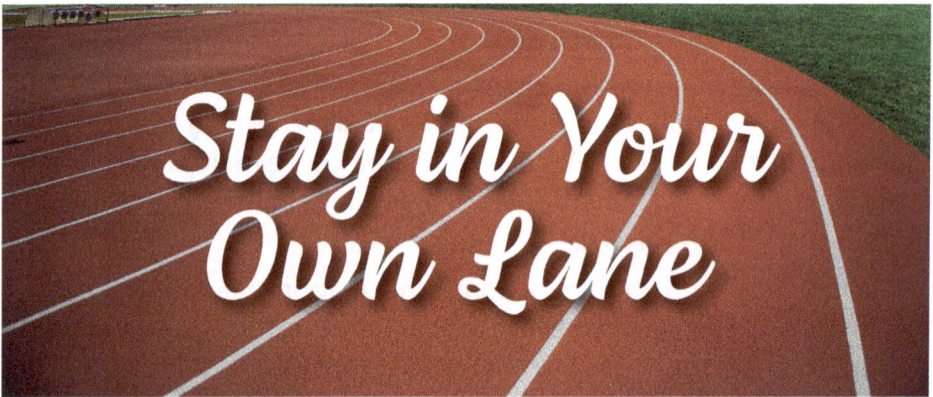

The last half of this chapter has almost read like a job description. The company has *XYZ* expectations of you. In return, you will receive *ABC* benefits from the company. We've seen a lot of the benefits we'll receive from God: He'll reconcile us, preserve us, make peace with us, deliver us, transfer us. In exchange, He expects that we'll continue, that we'll receive those blessings with thanksgiving. Part of Paul's message here is that we ought to stay in our own lane. It is not our job to deliver ourselves, or to transfer ourselves. It is not our job to reconcile ourselves or to make peace on our own with God. If we try to do any of those things, we'll fail utterly. Only Jesus can do them because He is so excellent and because He is the dwelling place of the fullness of God. Our job, then, is to be thankful and to continue. That's what God asks of us.

It's tempting to jump over into God's side of things. How many times have we studied with people who respond, *"Well, I just need to get my life together, then I'll come to Jesus"?* That's exactly backward! We come to Jesus, continue in faithfulness with thanksgiving, and He is the one who gets our life together!! I've often heard sisters discuss the anxiety they feel trying to get everything together, trying to be good enough to justify Jesus's sacrifice, hoping they do enough to squeak into heaven by the skin of their teeth. That statement alone is a statement of lack of faith in God's ability to do His job! Our job is to continue faithfully and thankfully. God's job is to deliver us to heaven. Let's do our job, and let Him do His!

Paul discusses two types of struggles in this section. The first is physical—he says he suffers in his flesh. Of course, historically, from the book of Acts, we know this was a frequent occurrence in Paul's life. He was often beaten, run out of town, and jailed for his preaching of the gospel. He says here in 1:24 that he suffers in that way for their sake. The reason he says this is that his suffering fills up what is lacking in Christ's afflictions.

This is a confusing statement. On the surface, it almost sounds like Paul is arguing that Christ's sufferings were insufficient to save, and so Paul needs to suffer some as well so that the salvation work is fully accomplished. Of course, that's not what Paul is saying at all. Instead, he recognizes that while Jesus's work to save all men is finished, there is more work that needs to be done for the sake of the body of Christ. Paul's perfectly willing to suffer, then, for the sake of the brethren. In fact, he says that's the job—the stewardship that God gave to him, to suffer so that people can fully know the word of God.

Paul's reason for being willing to suffer is his interest in the mystery. Paul refers to the mystery several times in his writing. In this instance, Paul is pretty clear in the way he defines it. He calls it Christ in you, the hope of glory. This is such a rich phrase, full of so much meaning! God's mysterious plan was that Christ would live in each of His followers and that being in us would give us cause to hope for glory! This mystery, and the explanation of it, is Paul's *why.* This is why Paul willingly suffers, why he keeps spreading his message even where it's unwelcome, and why he will eventually be willing to die. God has given him a job. Paul's job is to spread the knowledge of God's mystery.

He further elaborates on this in verses 28-29. He begins with something that could be viewed as his mission statement: *"Him we proclaim."* Paul's mission, his driving purpose in life, is to proclaim Christ. That's it. In order to accomplish this mission, he notes several things that he does: he warns, he teaches, he toils, he struggles. All of these actions work toward the goal he describes at the end of verse 28: he wants to do everything he can to present everyone mature in Christ.

What a succinct view of his life's work! Everything about Paul's life centers around his mission, his work, and his goal. He lives, eats, and breathes telling people about the gospel. Every waking moment is about what else he can do to present the people with whom he comes in contact as mature in Christ. This overriding sense of mission is an important learning point for us as well. We must be similarly mission-focused. We must work through warning, teaching, toiling, and struggling in order to accomplish our mission. We must keep our goal of presenting ourselves first and those around us second mature in Christ.

Keep in mind, too, that here Paul is still talking about his physical struggles. When we think of struggling for the gospel, our struggles typically involve what Paul hasn't even talked about yet—mental and emotional struggles, anxiety, and the like. Here Paul is still discussing physically suffering for the sake of the gospel. If we are to be similarly mission-focused, we must also be willing to accept not just social and emotional ramifications but physical consequences as well.

Paul changes subjects somewhat in the beginning of chapter two to discuss a different type of struggle. Here, Paul addresses the mental and emotional burden of his work in spreading the gospel. Specifically, we learn something about the church in Colossae. Paul says that he feels extra burdened on behalf of the Colossians, the Laodiceans, and all the other Christians he's never met. Paul's letter is going to a group of Christians he's never actually met in the flesh. Of course, this doesn't change the love in Paul's heart nor the love in his letter. Where we might tend to be a little less demonstrative with people we've never met, or a little more tight-lipped, Paul lays his love for them out there just like he would with any group of Christians. Even though he's never met them, he loves them dearly because they're brethren for whom Christ died.

When we think of mental and emotional struggles around preaching the gospel, we think of things like rejection or isolation. While I'm sure those weighed on Paul just like they do on us—after all, Paul was still a human—those emotional concerns aren't what he mentions in his letter to the Colossians. Instead, he talks about what he hopes for them. His soul is burdened, not by his own situation, but by his intense desires for the spiritual growth of the brethren in Colossae. He wants for them to have their hearts encouraged, for them to be close to one another

and bound together by love. We also see some repeated language from Paul's prayers for them in 1:10 and following. Here, Paul is in part reiterating what he's already told them about his prayers for them, but he is also adding the dimension of his own dedication to seeing those things happen for them. Paul prays for these things but also does his work in writing the letter to help them get to that point because he so desperately wants that fullness for them.

Of course, Paul has to remind them where their perfection will come from. It won't come only from their effort or only from Paul's writing. Instead, he mentions again that the wisdom and knowledge that they need to become complete and perfect are all in Christ. This goes back to Paul's repeated theme: redemption, salvation, and maturation as Christians come, not from the efforts of the people involved, but from the work of Christ within them and the grace of God. Even as Paul prays and shares the content of his prayers with the Colossians, he remembers the real worker in salvation—God is the one who saves.

Paul then explains his reasoning for his concern. He is concerned for all Christians, sure, but especially for those with whom he is not and has not been present in the flesh. He says he's worried that someone will delude them with reasonable-sounding arguments. What a fantastic thing to be worried about! It happens often and easily. Those who are new to the faith, who have a basic understanding, are especially likely to be swayed by someone who is close enough to the truth to sound reasonable. Paul is concerned that, without him among them to put a stop to it, they'll wander away from the faith because of deluding false teachers.

Really, Paul's concerns and prayers for the Colossians have a lot to teach us about how we should think about and pray for our brethren overall. I've often asked for prayers, and I've often been asked to pray for someone else. Frequently, those prayers are for physical health and well-being. Someone's mother is sick. Someone's spouse got a cancer diagnosis. More rarely, it'll be a request about dealing with some particular sin. *Brother so-and-so* has succumbed to his temptation to alcohol again. *Sister such-and-such* needs help withstanding the temptation to anger. Very rarely, if ever, have those requests been for greater heights of understanding. Infrequently do I get requests to pray for someone to have access to the riches of understanding and wisdom available in Jesus. This is frequently the content of Paul's prayers, though! We have much to learn about how to pray for our brethren.

Thought Questions

1. Write a summary of Colossians 1 as a job advertisement. Is it a job you'd take? Why or why not?

2. Skim through the book of Acts. What kind of physical suffering did Paul see for the gospel?

3. What is the mystery?

4. Why does Paul talk so much about the mystery?

5. Describe Paul's mission, action, and goal.

6. Describe your own mission, actions, and goal.

7. How do we feel about Christians we've never met?

8. How does Paul's prayer in Colossians inform how we should pray for our brethren and ourselves?

9. What do you think is the best approach to leading someone away from the pull of the works of the flesh?

Taken Captive
Colossians 2:6-15

Lesson 5: Taken Captive

Theological doctrine can be a difficult study. It's my experience that a lot of women, especially, shy away from heavy doctrine and theology in favor of application-based topical studies. Doctrine can be difficult to understand, the sentences difficult to parse, the concepts difficult to digest. The beginning of Colossians is rich with doctrine and theology! Paul covers everything from salvation to the deity of Jesus and plenty in between. At the beginning of 2:6, however, Paul signals a slight change in course. He begins the sentence with *"therefore."* In a nod to the truly awful humor of my high school English teachers, it's important to ask ourselves what the *"therefore"* is *there for*. What purpose does it serve? Why does it show up?

Paul has spent a while laying groundwork about Jesus and God and our salvation. Now he intends to turn to talking about what we do about that. The majority of the rest of the book will be application and righteous living rather than deep theology. Yet, that doesn't mean that Paul included the first part of the book just to check boxes and because he figured he probably ought to talk about God for a bit. Instead, the *"therefore"* indicates not only a change in subject, but a relationship between the two subjects. The application part of Paul's letter doesn't exist in a vacuum. Instead, it's directly related to all of the doctrine that he went to such pains to lay out at the beginning of the book! This functions not only as a connector but also as a reminder. By including his *"therefore"* clause, Paul is reminding us that all of the application points he'll go on to make are directly related to the study we did at the beginning of the book about the nature of Jesus, God, and our salvation. Remembering that will completely change how we see the applications Paul wants us to take from his letter.

The first real instruction that Paul gives to the Colossians, is *to walk.* We've seen this before. At the beginning of chapter 1, he indicated his desire for them to walk worthy. Here, though, they're just walking. Already, we're getting reminders of the important theology we learned in chapter 1. God is the One who makes us worthy, who strengthens and qualifies and transfers and delivers us. However, as Paul reminds the Colossians in 2:6, they still have to walk. God makes them worthy, but

they have to decide to put one foot in front of another. In an amusing word picture, Paul then goes on to tell them to be rooted, built up, established and abundant. Those words all suggest a tree, one with deep roots, a strong trunk, limbs that spread, and branches that bear fruit. Of course, the walking part of the instruction is a little at odds with this, but the picture of the tree is a compelling one. The learning that they've done and the fellowship and learning that they will continue to do will be what enables them to walk in Christ, based on everything they've received from Paul and from Christ.

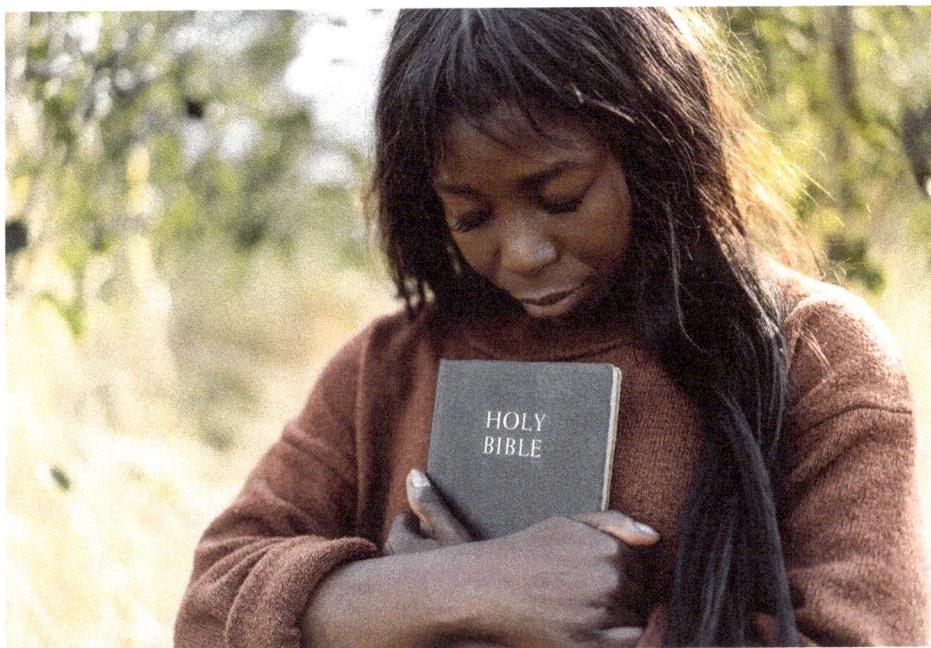

Of course, the rooted tree language is also significant to the warning Paul is about to deliver. When a tornado or hurricane comes through an area, one of the inevitable consequences is overturned trees. It's always interesting to see which trees remain standing and which ones topple when a strong wind hits. While established trees sometimes fall in the face of a tornado, younger trees do much more often. Younger trees don't have the well-established root system to hold them to the ground. They don't have strong trunks to stand tall rather than bending in the wind. While they may lose some limbs, more mature trees will stand to see another day. Paul is making the same point here. While the Colossian brethren can't help being young in the faith, they can focus on doing everything within their power to improve their root systems, to strengthen their trunks, to bear fruit while they're able, so that when the storm comes, they'll be better able to withstand it.

Paul then turns to discussing what he wants to warn them about specifically at this point in his letter. He tells them not to be taken captive. He worries about them being taken captive by philosophies, traditions, and elemental teachings that aren't according to Christ. Of course, philosophies and traditions aren't wrong in and of themselves. My family has a tradition of eating sweet potatoes rather than mashed potatoes with Thanksgiving dinner. Is there anything wrong with that? While you might not prefer it, Jesus doesn't have opinions on what we have for Thanksgiving dinner. However, being taken captive by philosophies and traditions becomes problematic when they involve topics upon which Jesus has taught!

While Paul has a specific philosophy in mind that he'll bring up in a moment, this is an important point for us as well. It's easy, especially for those young in the faith, but really for any of us, to be taken in by philosophies that sound reasonable. If we aren't sufficiently learned in what Christ has for us, we can learn of a philosophy or tradition that sounds reasonably close to what we know of the gospel and be taken captive. Of course, the answer to that problem is just a couple of verses up: *be rooted in Jesus.* If our roots are established and our growth is abundant, that will keep us from being taken captive just as it would the Colossian brethren.

In 2:9-10, Paul seems to jump tracks and go back to talking again about Jesus. We've seen descriptions of Jesus before, and some of this description of Jesus is familiar. Paul talks again about the whole fullness of deity being in Jesus. He talks about Jesus being the head of all authority. Both of these concepts establish Jesus as the supreme authority figure. This is relevant to the discussion at hand, of course, because if Jesus is just a man, just a teacher, just a leader, then He might have good ideas about what we should do, or He might not. If He's just a teacher, I can take some of His ideas that I think are good and incorporate them, and the ideas I'm not so keen upon I can reject.

If Jesus is the supreme authority, though, I don't get to decide what I think of His teachings. I must not be taken captive by philosophies that aren't in line with His teaching because He is God and is the head over whoever came up with those philosophies.

We also get some new descriptors of Jesus in this section, though. First, we get that Jesus is not just God, but that the whole fullness of deity dwells in bodily form in Him. This is not just a lowercase-g-god walking on the earth but God Himself dwelling in bodily form. To contemplate that at all is mind-boggling. Jesus is intended to be bigger than we can comprehend, and with good reason! A God that we can comprehend entirely, that we can wrap our minds around, is no God at all. Paul also presents Jesus as what makes us complete. This is yet another answer to those who would take Christians captive. I don't need new philosophies or additions to Jesus. Being in Jesus makes me perfect, complete, full. I need nothing more.

In order to be complete and full in Jesus, though, we have to be in Jesus. Paul describes two possible ways of accomplishing that. The first, the old covenant way of being attached to God, was through circumcision. The new covenant way, of course, is baptism. These two have a lot in common. Most significantly, both are signs of the covenant. They are the signature on the legal document, the final necessary step to entering the covenant with God. Both involve a partial putting to death. Both seem unrelated to the internal processes that they represent. Both are symbolic, which is a hugely important point. Is there anything about circumcision on its own that endears one to God? Is there anything about baptism on its own that endears one to God? Of course not! The significance of each action is because of the belief that the action represents, and more significantly, the significance is ultimately from the action of God on the basis of that belief.

This also reveals Paul's concern about the specific philosophy by which he fears the Colossians will be taken captive. There was a strong faction in the first century that insisted that in order to be a Christian, one must first become a Jew. In order to be a Christian pleasing to God, you also had to be circumcised, go to temple, engage in the sacrificial system, keep a kosher kitchen, etc. These Judaizing teachers, as they're called, are discussed in much of the New Testament. Part of Paul's point, then, in comparing circumcision and baptism is that if the Colossian brethren have been baptized, they've already entered the covenant! They don't need to be circumcised, or any other things God expected of Jews under the old covenant, because they're already in a covenant relationship with God. If circumcision and baptism are both ways in which one enters the covenant, then baptism takes care of it sufficiently!

Once we've entered the covenant, Jesus takes on a new and special role for us. That role is examined in 2:13-15. In those verses, Jesus forgives us. He cancels the record of our debt, sets aside legal demands,

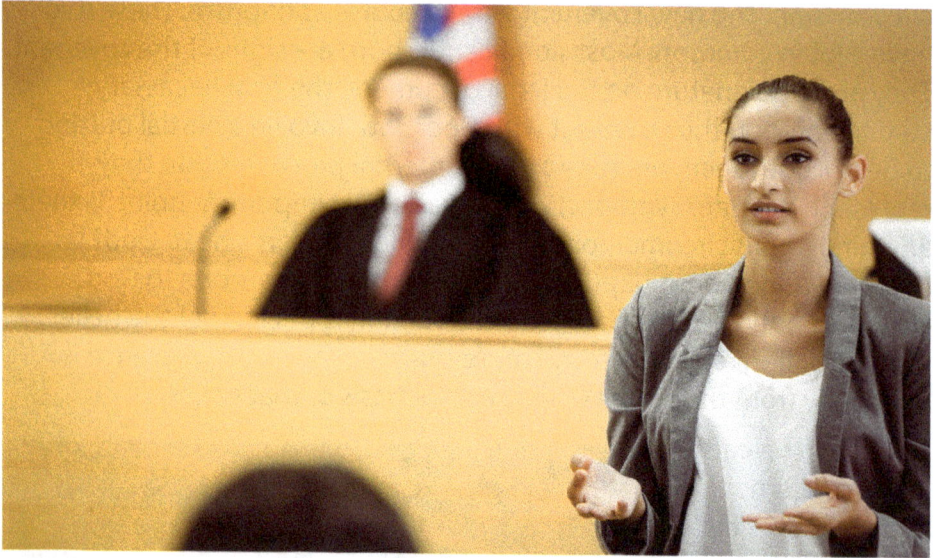

nails those demands to the cross, puts His enemies to open shame, and triumphs over them. That's quite a list! In my mind, this section plays out like an old episode of Perry Mason. Jesus is our defense lawyer. Satan thinks he's got us over a barrel. There are demands that we haven't met. We're without excuse. Then Jesus strides in and informs the court that He's canceled the record of our debt. He can do that because He took the demands that were placed on us and nailed them to the cross. He's forgiven us. In this forgiveness, at such cost to Himself, He puts the enemy to shame and triumphs over him. And in Jesus's triumph, we triumph as well! Jesus is more than just our defense attorney, though. He's a defense attorney who's highly motivated. He loves us so much that He was willing to take the payment of the debt on Himself to make sure we would walk out of the courtroom free. What a good God we serve!

Thought Questions

1. How does your reason for doing something change the way in which you do it? Give an example.

2. Consider Paul's tree analogy in 2:6-7. To what does each part correspond? Draw a picture.

3. What philosophies or traditions do you see now that sound reasonable, but that could take a Christian captive?

4. How has Jesus demonstrated to you that He's bigger than you are?

5. In what ways has being in Jesus completed and perfected you?

6. What similarities between circumcision and baptism do you see?

7. Are you in a covenant relationship with God? How do you know?

8. If Jesus has canceled your debt, how much influence should you allow those who would take you captive? Why?

Passing Judgment
Colossians 2:16-23

Lesson 6: Passing Judgment

The end of the last section almost seemed like a non sequitur. Paul was talking to the Colossians about being sure of what they were doing and about not being taken captive by reasonable sounding philosophies. Then, he launches into discussing what Jesus has done for them? On its face, that doesn't really make sense in context. As usual, though, Paul is connecting what he had been talking about and what he would talk about next by reviewing information he'd conveyed earlier.

Part of the Christian's walk in Jesus is being firm in who Jesus is and what Jesus has done. In a lot of ways, even for us, Christianity is an intensely personal journey. It is not really about the set of laws we keep *(though those are important)* or the actions we take *(also important)* or even the salvation offered by Jesus *(definitely also important)*. At its core, Christianity is about Jesus. If we are to be called by His name, He is the most important part of that calling. That means that in order to really be a Christian, we must be focused on Him. That will lead to a resistance on our part of being taken captive and swayed by philosophies that are opposed to Him and His teaching.

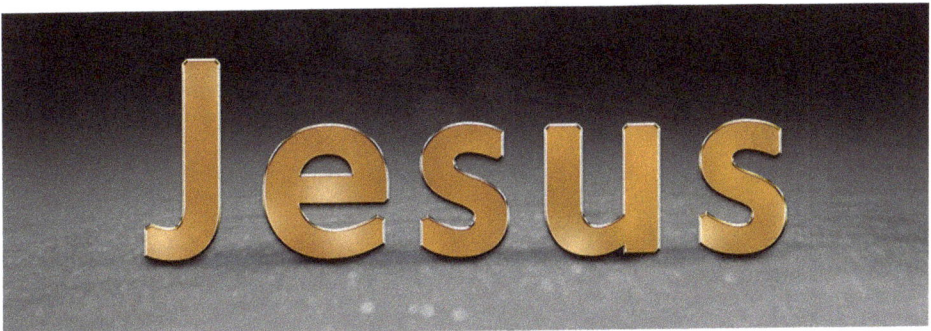

Of course, if we are focused on Him, that also changes our view of ourselves. Paul is about to start a discussion of passing judgment. This is a sensitive conversation even now, just as it was then. Part of what Paul wanted the Colossians to remember, then, going into a description of inappropriate ways that one might pass judgment on one's brethren, is that Jesus is sufficient. Jesus is enough. Jesus has done everything for you that you need in order to be made right before God. He is plenty.

In Colossians 2:16, Paul begins this section by telling the Colossians that they must not let anyone pass judgment on them. Specifically, he mentions a whole list of things that they shouldn't let people pass judgment on them about: food, drink, festivals, new moons, and Sabbaths. That's a lot. It's a short list, but there's a lot bound up in that list. Don't let anyone judge you about what you eat, what you drink, and a whole list of holy days. He then gives a reason why they shouldn't let people judge them for those. He says those are just a shadow of what was to come, but that the substance of those things belongs to Jesus.

As he so often does, Paul is coming at the same thing in a different way. He's talking again here about Judaizing teachers. All the things on the judgment list are associated with the practice of Judaism in the 1st century. Food and drink regulations, festivals, and Sabbaths are all contained in the old law. While new moon celebrations aren't in the law, by the beginning of Solomon's reign, those are a part of the Jews' religious observances, as they are referenced in 1 Chronicles 23. He's urging the Colossians not to let others judge them for not being observant Jews and for not keeping to the festival schedule and kosher regulations of Judaism.

His reason is that these regulations are a shadow. We see this language elsewhere throughout the New Testament, such as in Galatians 3:24, where Paul says that the law was a tutor to bring them to Christ. Paul's point is that the dietary and festival regulations of the old law had an important purpose. That purpose was to point the Jews *(and really the whole world)*, to Christ and His coming, and to prepare the world for Him. However, now that Christ has come, the restrictions that were meant to prepare are a mere shadow and not the actuality. They're not important anymore because of the work that Christ has already done.

Paul's not only talking about the Jews and Judaizing teachers, though. In 2:18, he turns to another type of false doctrine. He uses slightly different phrasing this time, urging the Colossians not to let anyone disqualify them. This is a little clearer than judging, to us. I can judge someone without presuming to decide their eternal destination. Disqualifying someone, though, means that these false teachers weren't just saying the Colossians were bad people, but that they weren't really full Christians.

This time, though, the ones disqualifying are doing so on the basis of a different teaching. Rather than judging based on their keeping of Judaism, these are judging based on Gnostic principles: special knowledge, angels, and asceticism. Gnosticism was another prevalent false teaching in the 1st century and beyond. This was just another version of saying that in order to be a real Christian, you had to do extra stuff on top of what Jesus required. It's the same basic process, just a different set of extra requirements.

This time, however, Paul also comments on what type of person goes around disqualifying others on the basis of their not holding to these beliefs. He says that this person is puffed up and that they're not holding fast to the Head. It's a pretty apt description, isn't it? To think that we know better than Jesus what's required of someone to make God happy is the very definition of being puffed up! Instead of thinking we know best, the way to redemption is to hold fast to the Head, which has been Paul's point all along.

Paul goes on to pose a couple of questions in verses 20 and 21. He asks them why, if they're dead to the world, are they acting as though the world still holds some power over them, in accordance with the world's demands? This is a question that plagues us as well. Just as the Colossians found, it's all too easy to die to the world, then forget that you've died and let the world go on calling the shots for you. For the Colossians, this showed up as trying to impress the religious elite around them with how well they can follow the rules.

Different rules apply to different situations. If you're in a different country, the rules of that country apply to you. If you're outside playing vs. inside playing, different rules apply. While pajamas are perfectly wonderful for wearing at bedtime, they're not usually the best choice for wearing to work. That's what Paul is telling the Colossians. "Things have changed! You've died to the world, so the rules have changed, and you have a new set of rules governing your behavior now. Don't be a zombie, still trying to live by the old rules even though you've died. Acknowledge your new life."

It's interesting that Paul comes at this problem from two separate angles. In the previous section, he condemned the people who were teaching this, the people who were trying to put extra requirements on

believers. Now, though, he's also fussing at the believers for falling for it. Part of Paul's message is that everyone involved in this false doctrine, the teachers of it and those who believe it, know better and ought to stop.

He elaborates further on this argument by talking about the rules that are being imposed on Christians. He says that all the rules have to do with things that perish with the using. Looking back at some of the things he specifically mentions, that's undeniably true. Food and drink are obviously in that category. Even things like festivals and celebrations fit that description. Do you remember everything you did three Thanksgivings ago? While there is a sense of lasting significance, there's also a sense that the things associated with celebrations are gone as soon as the celebration is over. Even concepts like asceticism *(strict denial of indulgence for religious reasons)* will pass away. Was your great-great-grandmother particularly indulgent or ascetic in her lifestyle? No one knows because that's not the kind of thing that people remember. Once the body is gone, so are the things associated with the body.

Of course, this isn't the case with the things that actually matter. No one wrangles over whether we ought to love one another more. They might wrangle over how to show that love but not over the love itself. No one argues about whether we need more patience. Maybe what that patience looks like, but not the patience. No one denies the need for more goodness or gentleness. The things that truly matter are things that are beyond the physical, things that don't perish with using, but instead grow as they're used more. Those are the things with which we ought to concern ourselves.

Paul reaches the climax of his argument in verse 23. Here, he insists that though all of these extra rules and regulations have the appearance of wisdom and religion, they're actually of no value in stopping self-indulgence. Read that again. Though they appear to be helpful and useful, they do NOTHING to make you a better person or get you closer to God. This is huge. This was mind-blowing for the Colossians, and it's mind-blowing for us. All these things that we think make us better people, these things that other people tell us will make us better people, don't actually work. All the self-help books about living your best life don't actually get you closer to Jesus, which is how to actually live the best life.

We can trust Paul when he says this, and not just because he's inspired by the Holy Spirit. If anyone would've been able to make self-made religion work for stopping fleshly indulgence, it would've been Paul. In Philippians 3, he lists his religious bona fides, and boy, does he have them! Paul was a truly impressive Jew, in the sense of keeping the Law and checking all the boxes for doing Judaism right. What did that get him? Nothing at all, until he found Jesus.

This reinforces one of Paul's major themes throughout the last few sections: the supremacy of Jesus. In 2:9-15, Paul made a thorough argument about the work that Jesus has done in us and for us. Jesus is where the fullness of deity dwells bodily, He's the head of authority, He's set aside the record of debt against us. He's over all things, and He's decided He wants us on His team. Because of that, the Colossians didn't need to worry about other people's expectations or requirements. Jesus had declared them saved and redeemed and transferred to His kingdom, and Jesus is the only one whose opinion matters!

Thought Questions

1. What in all of the descriptions of Jesus that we've seen so far most impresses you?

2. What things might people judge about today that are shadows and not substance?

3. What lesson do we learn from Paul's descriptions of various false doctrines?

4. Describe the person who judges based on extra requirements. Is this an attractive description?

5. What are some situations where we can be tempted to still live as though the world holds power over us?

6. Are the situations in question 5 about things that perish with using?

7. Can you think of a time when you've listened to Satan's lies about self-made religion getting you closer to Jesus?

8. Where in your life are you living as though Jesus isn't sufficient and you need to do more to save yourself? How can you change that?

Not on Earthly Things
Colossians 3:1-9

Lesson 7: Not on Earthly Things

Paul begins Colossians 3 with a significant phrase: *"If then".* This phrase indicates a connection with what came before. Paul has spent two chapters laying groundwork. He's started addressing a little application, but the beginning of chapter 3 is where the application really starts coming through. The first two chapters, then, are the groundwork. That groundwork changes everything! I have been guilty, sometimes, of passing over the theological groundwork in books like Colossians. It can be meaty and difficult to work through. Instead, I just skip on through to the application, get my *to-do list*, and go on my way.

"If then" in Colossians 3:1 says that's entirely the wrong way to go about it. The theology in the first half of the book might be a little meaty and difficult, but it changes the way we read the rest of the book. The rest of the book isn't a *to-do list* if we want to be saved. It's not a guilt-laden list of all the things we're doing wrong as Christians. Instead, it's a response. If God has saved us. If God has qualified, delivered, and transferred us through Jesus. If Jesus is the image of the invisible God, the Firstborn of all creation, the Creator of everything, the Head of the

body, the beginning, if the fullness of God dwells bodily in Jesus, if Jesus has presented us, if Jesus is in us, the hope of glory, if we are joined to Jesus in baptism, if Jesus is sufficient, then what?

The *then-what* is in Colossians 3:1, when Paul tells the Colossians to seek the things that are above. Immediately, we react with guilt and frustration. Okay, here's what I'm doing wrong. Here's what I need to be doing if I want to go to heaven. Yet, Paul is quick to tell us why we need to seek the things above. We seek the things above because that's where Christ is. If, presumably, all of the things in the first half of the book have happened because we chose them, then we should keep choosing! If we chose Jesus and chose to accept His deliverance and presentation of us, then we should continue to choose Jesus by seeking the things that are where He is.

He goes even further with it, though, when he says that the Colossians have died and their life is hidden with Christ. Everything in the book has been leading up to this. Everything has been about the work that Christ

has done for them. They have died to the world, and Jesus has brought them back to life. If that's true, then Paul's point is that God owns them. God has bought them and has given them life. Jesus worked hard to give them the life that they've gained. Because of that, they owe their life and existence to God. They are slaves to God, to Jesus, and that means that God calls the shots for what they do with their lives. Paul reminds them, though, that if they are true to the purpose for which God raised them to new life, they'll be rewarded for that. When Jesus returns, those who are His will be glorified along with Him.

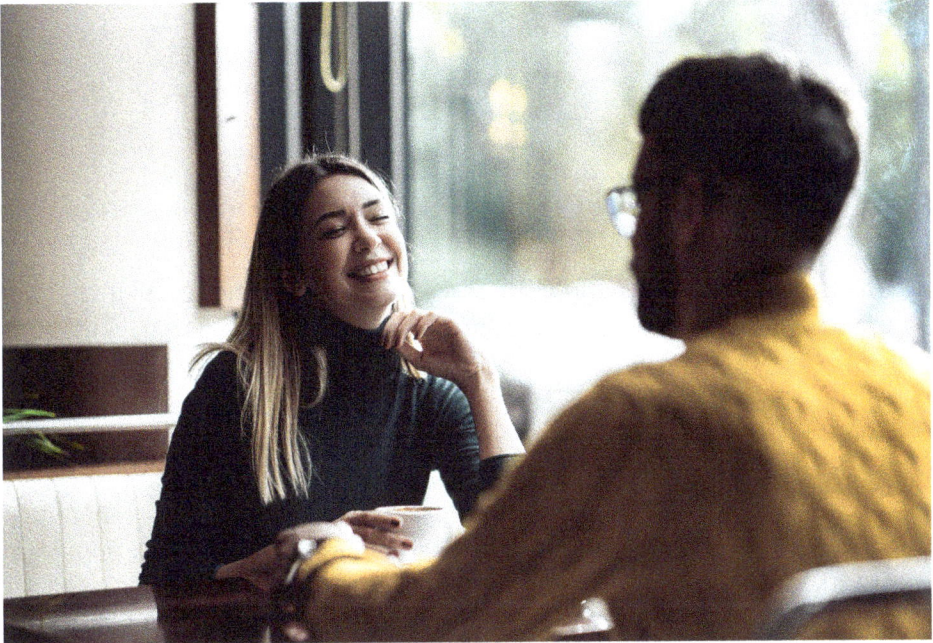

Paul continues with the life-and-death language in verse 5 by telling the Colossians to put some things to death. Specifically he tells them to put to death what is earthly within them and then gives a list of examples: sexual immorality, impurity, passion, evil desire, and covetousness. This isn't intended to be a comprehensive list of every sin from which they should abstain; Paul gives another list just a couple of verses later. Why then does Paul include these items together and not other items?

The common thread through all of these items is the passion in them. They are all certainly sexual sins, though some of them aren't exclusively sexual in nature. Passion includes sexual sin but can also include other things. These sins are involve a lack of self-control, and frequently a willful lack. Most of these are not just losing self-control but deliberately choosing to throw self-control out the window.

Paul also mentions that these sins are to be put to death because the wrath of God is coming because of them. This is intended to intimidate and scare the Colossians. While certainly God is a God of love and kindness, He's also the Living God, and it's a fearful thing to fall into His hands. This is also intended to distinguish God from the pagan gods of the cultures around them. Many of the pagan gods were worshipped by sexual immorality and a loss of control. Paul is making sure that the Colossians are aware that God is not to be worshipped with such things, but with self-controlled behavior instead.

We then learn something that feels shocking about the Colossian brethren. Paul says that the Colossians once walked in these sins. He says this in a very matter-of-fact fashion. This feels alarming. We do not like to acknowledge our own previous sin so baldly, much less talk plainly about someone else having engaged in such things. The problem is, while I didn't engage in sexual immorality before coming to Christ, I absolutely indulged my passions and evil desires. I just don't like to talk about that. If I don't talk about it, then I can pretend it doesn't exist. Paul isn't allowing us that evasion. This seems objectionable to our sensitivities, but it's such an important part of our walk with Christ!

All of Paul's discussion in the book so far has been around Jesus saving the Colossians *(and us)* from the sins that separated them from God.

However, the whole plan falls apart if we don't sin. Of course, all of us sin. However, if we somehow didn't have sin, we wouldn't need Jesus, and His sacrifice would have been in vain. If we haven't done anything wrong, we can't be forgiven for it. As a corollary, if we aren't willing to acknowledge our sins, we can't ask forgiveness for them. We have to be willing to openly admit the sins we've committed if we want to receive forgiveness for them.

Verse 8 starts a new list of sins that Paul wants the Colossians to avoid. This isn't because Paul forgot to include these in the first list, and so he just tacked on another list a bit later. Instead, there are important thematic differences between the two lists. While the list in verse 5 involves sins of passion and mostly sexual behavior, the list in verse 8 has much more to do with sins of the tongue. Paul includes anger, wrath, malice, slander, and obscene talk on the list. While this is definitely a different type of list, there's much about it that's the same as the previous one. They all still represent a loss of self-control. They also demonstrate selfishness.

However, there are some differences. This list has to do with the heart and the way it is demonstrated in the way a person speaks. It also is much more *other-focused* than the first. Anger, wrath, malice, and slander all demand an object, and usually that object is a person.

A final sin of the tongue that gets its own mention is lying, in verse 9. This isn't a change in subject, even though it's a new sentence. Lying definitely fits in the category with the sins mentioned in verse 8. However, especially in our culture, lying is the most acceptable sin on either list. There are people who'll disapprove of everything on the lists, except lying? *"Come on; everyone lies. It's fine!"*

That's why lying needs its own discussion here. Lying is socially acceptable, it's easy, and it's just as offensive to God as any of the rest of it. It's also just as much an issue for our culture as it was for the Colossians. Paul warns them by including lying with other sins of the tongue.

Thought Questions

1. What do you think the "if" refers to in 3:1?

2. What falls into the category of things above?

3. What falls into the category of things below?

4. How does your life look different because your life has been hidden with Christ?

5. What do you think the wrath of God coming would look like?

6. Are there sins you refuse to acknowledge, even privately? Can you be forgiven for those?

7. How do we respond when a sister confesses to anger, wrath, or obscene talk? How should we respond?

8. What applications can we make from the inclusion of lying on the list of sins of the tongue?

Seek Things Above
Colossians 3:10-14

Lesson 8: Seek Things Above

As Paul moves his attention from not seeking things below to actively seeking things above, he uses lying as a turning point in the conversation. In 3:9, he instructed the Colossians to stop lying to each other. We're very familiar with instructions to stop doing something. We tell our kids all the time what *not to do*; laws are frequently phrased as what *not to do.* Even in the Bible, God's commandments are often set up as what we shouldn't do.

However, sometimes just focusing on what we shouldn't do makes it more difficult to stop doing that thing. If I tell you not to think about pink unicorns what are you thinking about now? Yep, pink unicorns! If we tell our brains not to think about something or do something, it can

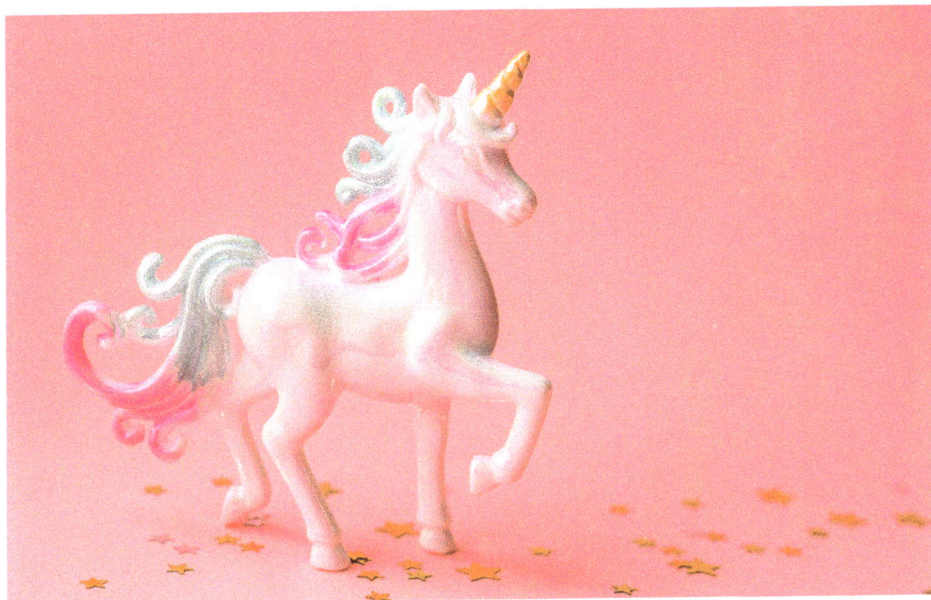

often make it harder because we've given our brain the prompt. So, in verse 10, Paul elaborates. He doesn't just tell the Colossians to quit lying and to take off the old self. Instead, he gives them something new to do, something constructive to focus on instead.

Here, Paul tells them not just to take off the old man, but to put on the new self. In fact, he even goes further, and says that they need to stop lying because they already have taken off the old and put on the new. If they've put on their new self, then the pieces of their old self won't work anymore. Paul is using the analogy of taking off clothing and putting on new clothing. He says, first, that their new man is being renewed in knowledge. They're not putting on dirty old clothes. These are new clean clothes that are constantly being renewed—made fresh again— by the Colossians' increased knowledge and learning.

These new clothes are also fashioned in the image of their Creator. If I were going to dress up in a costume to look like a princess, I couldn't just wear the same old clothes I always wear. I'd have to change my clothing, change my hair, and change my makeup. I'd have to change my voice, the way I walk, and maybe even things like my height. If I'm

going to look like someone, I have to change myself to look like them. I can't just tell people that I look like Kate Middleton! If I still look like my same old self, they're not going to be convinced. Similarly, if we're going to call ourselves by the name of Christ, we need to change our clothes, so to speak, so that we look like Him!

Colossians 3:11 is a familiar verse. It's beloved by many who are searching for unity, and rightly so. Paul goes through several opposed categories—Greek and Jew, slave and free—and says that those distinctions are no more, but that Christ is in all. People will run with this verse to insist that whatever we find to divide us—be it race, socioeconomic status, nationality, gender, politics, pizza preferences, or whatever else—shouldn't be a division. This is a worthwhile application. The things that divide us now, in our culture, ought not divide us, at least those of us who call ourselves Christians.

However, Paul's point here goes back to his point about putting on the new man. When you put on the new man, he argues, you're no longer Greek or Jew; you're no longer slave or free; you aren't those things anymore because the clothing you're wearing is renewing you in the image of your Creator. That means that not only should you not let those things divide you from others, you shouldn't let those things define you anymore, either. Who I am, at the most basic level, is no longer bounded by my race or ethnicity or socioeconomic status. Who I am is a new creature that belongs to Jesus. That's why Paul points out that Jesus is all and is in all. Jesus is the only part of my identity that matters, that exists, once I put on Christ.

The clothing analogy continues in Colossians 3:12. Paul starts to tell the Colossian brethren what they are to put on. He doesn't stop with the generic instruction to put on the new man; he tells them what the new man ought to look like. He reminds them first that they are God's chosen ones. They aren't Jews or Greeks or slaves or free. They're God's chosen ones. Their identity is totally wrapped up in Jesus and who He makes them to be.

This is a significant concept! Self-worth is sometimes a difficult thing to grapple with, especially for women. Our culture is constantly signaling us and reminding us about all the ways in which we fall short. We're too tall or too short. We're too fat or too skinny. We're too smart or too dumb. We're too conservative or too liberal. We're too rich or too poor. Sometimes it feels like a good balance is impossible to find in one

category, much less all of them! Paul's message here is that your concept of self isn't going to rely anymore on outside indicators, or really on anything that you do. Going back to some of the earliest concepts in the book, reminding them that God is the One who saves, Paul again tells them that God is the One who assigns value.

You are no longer a Jew striving to keep the law perfectly so that you can be pleasing, yet never measuring up. You are no longer a Greek serving the whims of a capricious false god. You are no longer free to devise your own course through life. You are no longer a slave to someone who owns your body and your labor. Instead, you are the chosen one of God! You are holy and beloved! Now, Paul says, act like it!

He outlines eight characteristics that he wants the Colossian brethren to put on. The first is a heart of compassion. This is a heart that feels for those around them, that sees the pain in the people with whom they associate. Compare this to the heart of one who indulges in anger and malice, earlier in this chapter. This is the heart that wants what's best for those around them, not out of a sense of duty, but because they genuinely care for those people.

Next is kindness. Compare this to the mean-spirited list in 3:8. This is also opposed to the impurity of the list earlier in the chapter, which uses people for one's own purposes rather than doing what is best for them. Kindness is looking for ways to treat others well, to go out of our way to do for someone else.

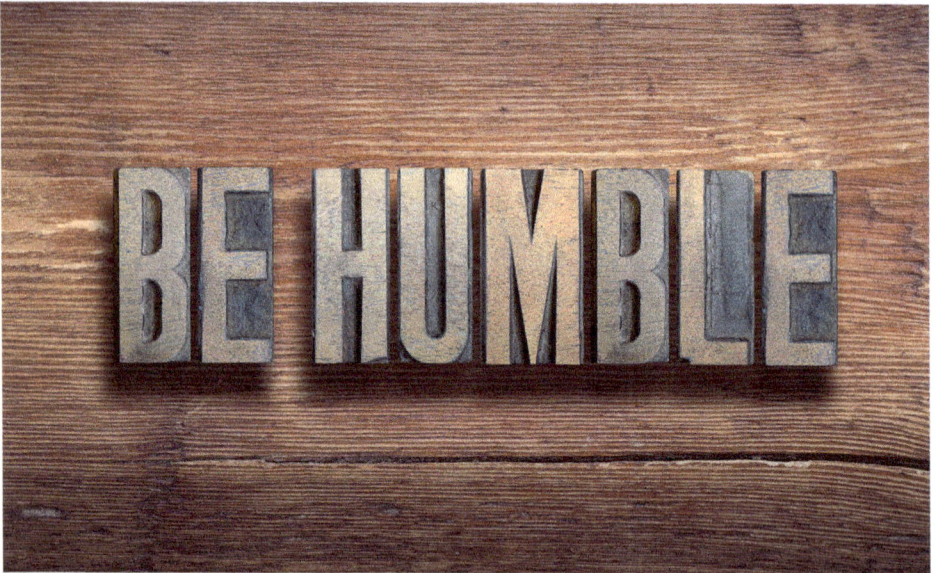

Next on the list is humility. This is the heart that does not seek its own, but seeks to benefit and exalt others. Contrast this with the one who slanders and lies about others to gain benefit. The humble heart happily puts others ahead of itself because it is assured of its own worth from God rather than needing to demean others in order to feel better about itself.

After humility is meekness. Where humility is about how you think of yourself with regard to others, meekness is about not insisting on getting your own way. Meekness is opposed to things like evil desire and covetousness. Meekness is willing to let someone else lead and do things his or her way because meekness knows that regardless, God will take care of us and make sure that the meek person has what she needs.

Next is patience. Patience is willing to wait, and not just to wait, but to wait happily and contentedly. Compare this with all of the sins on the lists earlier in the chapter. All of those sins involve a lack of patience in some way or another. Patience is about trusting God's timing and not insisting on what you want when you want it, knowing that God will do what is best when it is the best time for it.

The sixth item on Paul's list is bearing with one another. This characteristic is one that sees something differently than a brother or sister, but rather than impatiently stomping around demanding immediate change, is willing to let that brother or sister be whom he or she is, rather than needing others to conform entirely to us. Compare this to the wrath and malice in 3:9. Rather than grinding your teeth every time *sister so-and-so* loudly voices her opinion about the topic on which you disagree so strongly, bearing with lets go of the grudge and is content to let *sister so-and-so* have her own opinions.

Similar to bearing with is forgiving. Bearing with implies a difference of opinion but not sin or wrongdoing. Forgiving is about wrongdoing. If a brother has sinned against you, you must forgive. That's what God is calling the Colossians *(and us)* to do. Compare this forgiving spirit to the malice and slander in Paul's earlier list. If someone has wronged us in some way, our response need not be to form a mob and come after him with pitchforks and torches. Instead, the godly response to a slight is to forgive, not only because our identity can easily withstand being slighted, but also because we have been forgiven so much.

Finally, Paul calls the Colossians to love. This all-encompassing word is so popular in our time, but so few understand what it actually means and what it looks like. None of the sins on Paul's earlier lists are loving; in fact, sin is never loving. Instead, to avoid sin, our defense must be not merely to avoid committing those particular offenses against our brother, but to actively love him, and when we actively love our sister, we will avoid sinning against her.

Thought Questions

1. What are some reasons to keep lying out of the life of the Christian? Think of both negative *("Don't do this")* and positive *("Do this thing")* reasons.

2. What new behaviors have you used to replace the *old-you* behaviors that you took off so you could put on Jesus?

3. What identifiers have you taken off because of your new identity in Christ?

4. How does being a chosen one of God affect your self-worth and self-image?

5. For each of the eight characteristics that Paul encourages the Colossians to put on, think of a situation you've seen where that characteristic was necessary.

The Peace of Christ
Colossians 3:15-17

Lesson 9: The Peace of Christ

Whew. The last couple of lessons have been heavy with *do-and-do-not lists*. Women react especially strongly to such lists. When confronted with an overwhelmingly long and impossible-to-complete list of tasks, many women go into robot mode. Turn off thinking, turn off feeling, just do. Go and do the things that show you have a compassionate heart. Go and do the things that show you are meek. Go and do the things that show you aren't angry.

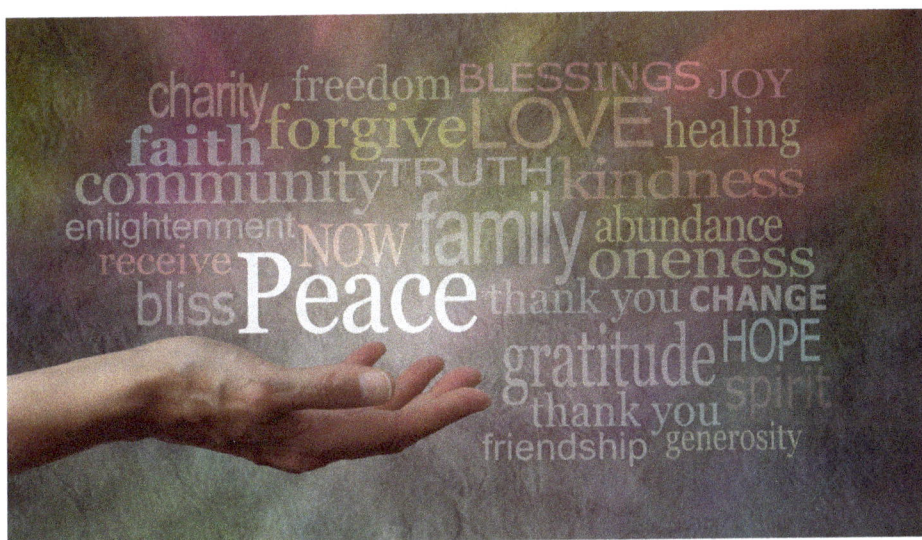

It's worth taking a minute here to remember the context in which these lists occur. Remember that Paul begins chapter 3 with an "if" statement. If God has done this wonderful work in you, if you are already saved, if you have let Jesus cancel the record of debt that was against you, and you now stand free thanks to His efforts, you don't have to check off the *to-do list* in order to prove your worth or earn your keep. This is the way God wants you to live because you've been saved, not in order to be saved. The pressure to live perfectly is off!

Paul starts the next section with an encouraging message. He tells the Colossians to let the peace of Christ rule in their hearts. The verb choice is interesting. This isn't *"be at peace"* or *"find peace."* This is "let." Allow. Jesus wants desperately to give you His peace, but He won't force it on you. You have to let Him in. Even in this instruction, Paul is urging the Colossians to stay in their own lane and let God do His job. A person trying to find or make his or her own peace is doomed to fail. There's too much working against it. The only way for us to have peace in this life is to bring God's peace into our own lives.

Of course, on its face this instruction seems counterintuitive. We think, *"Paul, you just gave me a whole big pile of things to do. Now you want me to be at peace? I can't be at peace; I'm far too busy!"* There are several problems with that approach. First of all, peace only looks counterintuitive in the face of Paul's instructions in verses 12-14 if those verses are a high-pressure, Old-Law-style list of what must be done to earn salvation. If the list in verses 12-14 is actually a list of ways to live to show your gratitude, the peace of Christ is a lot more possible in coexistence with a *to-do list* like that!

Grateful

Another problem with seeing peace as at odds with the calling of verses 12-14 is found in Paul's description of their calling in verse 15. He doesn't stop with telling them to let Christ's peace rule in their hearts. He tells them that they were called to the rule of Christ's peace and that this calling was in one body. Here Paul is returning to his common theme of unity. God has called them to be ruled by peace, and that calling occurs is one unified body. That unity is possible because of peace. As Paul told them in verse 12 of this chapter, Christ is all and is in all. Because of that unity through Christ, true peace can be found because Christ is the only important thing.

If Paul asking the Colossians to let Christ's peace rule them wasn't enough, he finishes up that verse with a simple instruction to be thankful. Be thankful for what? To whom? Why? Thankfulness is such an important part of the Christian's walk! Specifically here, Paul is talking about thankfulness for the peace of Christ that's going to rule in their hearts. However, in a bigger sense, being thankful is a fitting end to the list of characteristics of the life of the new man.

There is so much that Paul has mentioned in this book for which the Colossians can be thankful. In fact, a life of thanksgiving is reflective of the many blessings that God rains down on Christians. Keeping a sense of gratitude also makes it easier to retain the other characteristics in the list. If you are constantly thanking God for the good things in your life, for the blessings He's given, it's much easier to be kind, compassionate, forgiving. It's also impossible to let the peace of Christ rule your heart without thankfulness. If you are thankful, seeing God's blessings everywhere, then you will receive the peace that Christ offers as another blessing to you. If you refuse gratitude, then you won't see the peace of Jesus for the blessing that it is.

Thankfully, Paul also details how this peace comes about. Sometimes verses like this can be overwhelming—how do I just let it rule my heart? What does it look like? How do I know if I'm letting the right thing rule? What if I get it wrong? Paul is quick to reassure the Colossians about how they'll find the peace so that it can rule their hearts. When he instructs in verse 16 to let the word of Christ dwell in them richly, he's not sticking in a *by-the-way* proof text about the use of instrumental music in worship. He's still talking about the same thing! The way to clothe yourself with the new man, the way to let the peace of Christ rule you, the way to be thankful, is to let the word of Christ dwell in you!

This dwelling in you is not like letting your least favorite nephew crash on your couch for a couple of nights when he comes through town. This is not grudging or limited in time and access. The way Paul describes this dwelling is "richly." Let the word dwell richly in you. How do we accomplish that? Rich dwelling takes desire. You need to want that rich dwelling. It takes time. This rich dwelling is not the kind of thing that happens from a *once-a-week* brush with a sermon as you're playing Candy Crush while you listen. This rich dwelling requires an investment of your time and of yourself, but the rewards for this investment are great!

Those of us from an a cappella music background are incredibly familiar with this verse. I could quote Colossians 3:16 nearly as early as Ephesians 6:1. This is the text that we use to justify an exclusively a cappella song worship in our churches, and rightly so. That is a good, true, and appropriate application of this text. However, that's not what this text is actually about. In context, Paul is not talking about organs and praise bands. Of course he's not! What he's talking about is what a life lived as a new man looks like, how we change because of our new clothing, how our behavior changes because of our thankfulness, and, in this case, how our teaching methods and conversation methods change because of our membership in the body of Christ.

This passage is actually about what our song worship should look like, but not really just in the particular of whether we use instruments. A much more important point made by this Scripture is that our song worship ought to teach. The text is pretty specific that the actions we're to take with our song worship are to teach and admonish. This is a difficult point to consider at times. Music is designed by God to stir the senses and the emotions. It is right when we are emotionally moved by a song that we use to worship. However, that emotional experience shouldn't be the goal of our worship. Instead, the goal is stated at the very beginning of the verse: our song worship should be an avenue to letting the word dwell richly in us.

Imagine going to your favorite Chinese restaurant and ordering sweet and sour shrimp, and when it comes to the table, there's plenty of

sugar, breading, and rice but only three shrimp! Is the shrimp dwelling richly in your dish? We should have the same mindset when it comes to song worship. A bit of Bible is better than none, but I want my worship absolutely swimming in Bible! Filled to the brim! That is when the word of Christ will start dwelling richly, and when I'll be able to teach and admonish my brethren and be taught and admonished by them.

Paul finishes up this section with another familiar instruction. He tells the Colossians that whatever they do, they need to do it in the name of Jesus. Whether they're engaging in words or deeds, those need to be in Jesus's name. This doesn't mean just tacking on "In Jesus Name, Amen" at the end of prayers or throwing a "Lord willin'" on the end of a statement of intent. Instead, to do something in Jesus's name is to do it by His authority and to His glory. Paul is giving them a simple but difficult directive. His summary of the entire section on putting on the new man and seeking that which is above is right here. Everything the Colossians do or say needs to be something of which Jesus would approve; something that brings Him glory and honor.

This fits right in with the rest of the book, doesn't it? After all that God has done for us, after the supreme sacrifices that Jesus has made, our new man, new self, new life is dedicated to serving Him. Because of that, He gets to call the shots on what we do. As the last lesson demonstrated, He calls the shots on what our character looks like and how we behave. In this section, He calls the shots on what our mental state looks like, what our worship looks like, and everything else—everything we do or say. This seems like a lot, but given all that He's given us, is it, really?

The end of this section circles back around to thanksgiving. This time, it's paired with doing all in the name of Jesus. Thankfulness is always important, but, it fits well in this section especially. It's easy to see doing all in the name of Jesus as a chore or a burden. I don't ever get to do what I want to do. I've got to run everything by the Bible first. What a drag! In reality, when we have a grateful heart for everything Paul has already talked about in the book, doing all according to what Jesus wants us to do is a joy! How delightful to be able to please the One who has so blessed every part of our lives! That is how an attitude of thanksgiving changes the game.

Thought Questions

1. How did you feel coming face to face with the *to-do lists* in the last couple of lessons?

2. What roadblocks have you put up that are preventing Jesus's peace from ruling in your heart?

3. Where have you seen Christ calling you to His peace?

4. What are you thankful for in your walk with Jesus?

5. What would a rich dwelling of the word look like in you?

6. What favorite hymns allow the word to dwell richly within you?

7. To what part of your life does the admonition of 3:17 apply? Do you have an easier time in some parts of your life than others?

8. How easy is it for you to see doing all in the name of the Lord as a joy rather than a burden?

Submit
Colossians 3:18-4:1

Lesson 10: Submit

Paul has spent most of Colossians 3 detailing the ways in which a Christian ought to live their lives. While the list seems daunting, he tells the Colossians to live for Jesus with the peace that Jesus puts in their hearts, to let Him rule with that peace, and to be thankful for it. What a relief to let Jesus rule our hearts and to relish the peace that His rule brings! Then, of course, Paul has to go back to the *to-do lists* with an old favorite: submission.

Many a ladies' class, many a marriage class has foundered on the discussion of submission. It's an incredibly unpopular topic in our culture, at least in part because of misunderstanding. I had a conversation with a woman one time who insisted that she didn't go for that submission thing, *"no ma'am,"* that wasn't how her marriage operated. I asked how that looked, if a decision needed to be made and they disagreed, what happened? Well, of course, her husband was the head of the house and had the ultimate authority in decision-making for their family. I opted not to tell this dear lady that she was showing submission to her husband.

Contrary to popular belief, though, submission isn't just for wives. Paul spends the rest of chapter 3 and the first bit of chapter 4 talking through several roles in which submission is important. Paul is also careful to

leave space for individual relationships. Nowhere does Paul say, "Person A, submit to Person B, which will always look exactly like this." I've had young women tell me that there was no way they could get married because they'd seen their parents' relationship, and if that's what submission looked like, they weren't interested. Of course, my response was that just because that's what submission looked like for her parents, that wasn't necessarily what submission would look like for her. Every relationship looks different.

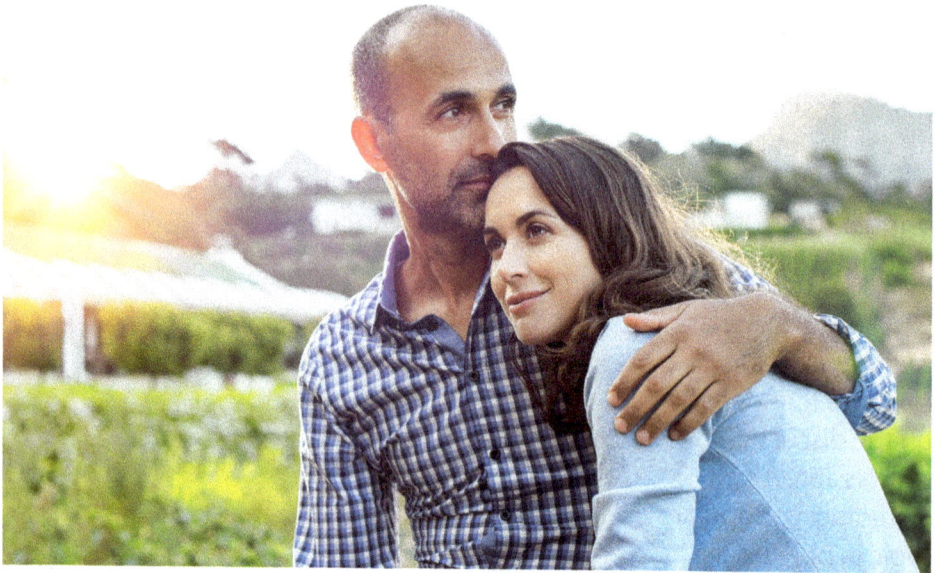

First, in Colossians 3:18, Paul tells wives to submit to their husbands. This is, of course, one of the two most famous submission relationships tied in familiarity with children obeying their parents. He tells wives to do this, simply, because it is fitting in the Lord. In other places in the New Testament, Paul goes into much more detail about some of the reasoning behind God's decision to put man as the head of the household. Here, he just describes the submission as fitting. There is a rightness, an appropriateness, to a woman who willingly and cheerfully submits to her husband. There is a wrongness, an inappropriateness, to a women who tries to control her husband with power plays, who sulks and grumbles about doing what needs to be done, who gossips about her husband to her friends at church so as to diminish him in the eyes of others.

Paul doesn't stop with wives being submissive, though. In 3:19, he tells husbands to love their wives and to avoid being harsh with them. Well, of course, that's different from submission. Love is a different word than submission. In reality, though, this self-sacrificial love is just another kind of submission. This is the kind of submission where a husband puts his wife's needs above his own, where he is gentle with her, and where he values her for her unique identity in Christ. Just as there is wrongness to the wife who tries to control her husband with power plays, there is a similar wrongness to a husband who controls his wife with power and intimidation rather than with love.

Next, Paul moves on in Colossians 3:20 to tell children to obey their parents. He instructs them to do this because it pleases the Lord. We talked a lot in the last lesson about viewing the *to do lists*, not as a bunch of work to earn your salvation, but as a way to live that pleases the One who's given so much for you. Paul gives the same rationale here for children being obedient. Certainly, children are frequently not pleased with obeying their parents. Sometimes, even parents are not pleased with requiring obedience from their children. At times, it's much easier in the moment to just let a child do what she wants! However, children obeying their parents is pleasing to the Lord.

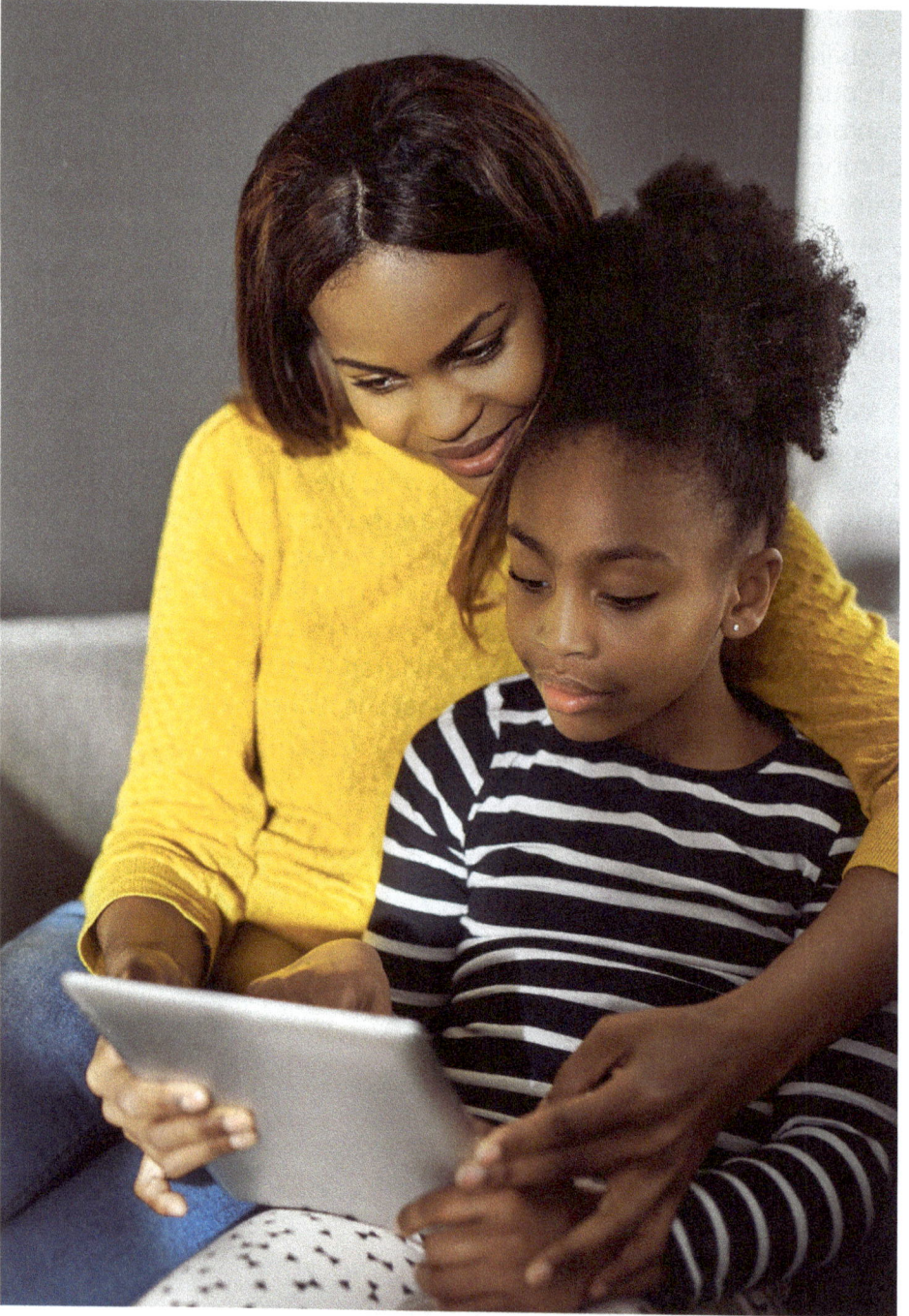

The next instruction Paul offers is to fathers in 3:21, when he tells them not to provoke their children. Of course, since we're not fathers, this has nothing to do with us, so we can skip right over this verse. Unfortunately, even though Paul addresses this one specifically to fathers, there's application for mothers here, as well. Parents generally must be careful not to provoke or exasperate their children. There are many forms this provocation can take. Sometimes it's harping on every last thing that they do wrong. Sometimes it might be inappropriate expectations for their behavior. It might have to do with grades, sports excellence, or physical appearance. Whatever form the provocation takes, though, Paul warns about the danger of children becoming discouraged. We've seen this before, haven't we? A parent is so determined to bring their child up right, in whatever sense, that they ignore the child himself and end up discouraging the child and driving the child away. While children must be taught and must obey, discouraging the child serves no one in the long run.

Paul has dealt with husbands and wives, and with children and parents. The final pairing begins with a discussion of bondservants. This is also the longest discussion aimed at a particular category of people. Beginning in Colossians 3:22, he tells bondservants to obey their masters in everything. While none of us are servants, application can

certainly be made to the employer-employee relationship. Employees ought to be submissive to their employers. Paul even goes further in the rest of the verse, describing the obedience of the bondservant as not merely outward service, but sincere submission.

In some ways, the discussion of behavior at work is even more difficult than the discussion of submission to a husband. Not only do I have to do what I'm told, but I have to work energetically and with a sincere heart? I have to actually submit myself to my employer, and not just do the least I can get away with without getting fired? This, too, is a counter-cultural instruction. In modern American culture, lying to your boss about being sick because you want to go do something else that day is common and considered a trivial thing. Paul tells the Colossians that such an attitude must not be common among Christians.

He explains why the bondservant would behave this way at the end of verse 22. The bondservant obeys her master with a sincere heart because she fears the Lord. Here Paul finds the meat of his arguments about submission. In 3:23-24, Paul discusses the importance of working for God, no matter what you're doing for whom. His reasoning is that when you're working for a master or an employer you're not actually working for that person. When I go to work teaching for a school, I'm not actually working for that school district. I'm working for the Lord.

That distinction seems trite, but its significance is huge. If I'm actually working for God, then even if my employer doesn't realize I'm scrolling social media while my students do their worksheet, my actual employer is fully aware. If I'm actually working for God, then even if my husband does something that I think is deserving of my scorn and passive aggressive attitude, the Lord hasn't, and He is the One I'm submitting to.

When we center God in all of our relationships, submission actually becomes much easier. I'm not submitting to my employer or my husband, I'm submitting to the God who loves me and is good and has done so much for me already.

Finally, in Colossians 4:1, Paul finishes the last pairing by addressing masters. While the natural analogy to draw is employers, Paul's instruction here also applies to the parent-child relationship. He tells masters to treat their servants justly, because the master has a Master of his own. This instruction addresses the *all-too-easy* trap of thinking that because we have people over whom we have authority, we're something special. It's easy to let that power go to our heads and think we have some measure of control, and so we can use that control to make people do whatever we want.

Instead, Paul urges fair and just treatment of those under our rule. While we may have authority over our employees or our children, there is One who still has authority over us. Jesus discusses the concept of receiving as you have given and being judged as you have judged in the Sermon on the Mount. The same principle applies here. Our Master is well aware of our doings and interactions with those under our authority, and just as Paul mentioned at the end of the section on bondservants, God shows no partiality. If we treat those under our authority with disrespect and contempt, God will avenge that wrong.

While Paul presents all of these as separate relationships, there is considerable overlap in all of these instructions to submit. Ultimately, all of the submission goes back to letting the peace of Christ rule in your hearts. When you are secure and content in God's work in you and your value because of it, submission is no problem. Submission does not degrade you because nothing can, after God has paid such a price for you! No matter which side of which relationship you're on, submission goes back to resting in Jesus.

Thought Questions

1. Did the peace we found at the end of the last lesson dry up with a discussion of submission? Why is that?

2. What does submission have to do with letting the peace of Christ rule your heart?

3. What does submission look like to you, generally? What specific parts of submission do you struggle with?

4. What has helped you learn to cheerfully submit to authority?

5. How do submission, love, and obedience connect with each other?

6. How have you provoked your children? Do you remember being provoked as a child?

7. How does working for the Lord change the way you work in earthly relationships?

8. How does remembering that you have a Master, as well, change the way you interact with those over whom you have authority?

Prayer and Wisdom
Colossians 4:2-6

Lesson 11: Prayer and Wisdom

Paul seems to change subjects pretty abruptly in Colossians 4:2, moving from a discussion of submission and earthly relationships to a discussion of prayer. Of course, Paul isn't actually abruptly switching topics. First, this is a further elaboration on his topic heading in Colossians 3:1, when he says that if we are raised with Christ, our lives will look different, and we will seek the things of Christ. Everything in the back half of the book, from submission to prayer to language to lying, is about conforming our lives to Jesus.

Additionally, though, a focus on prayer is really just another discussion of submission. It's tempting, in the absence of prayer, to think ourselves self-sufficient, to think that we're self-made. We can stroll along through our lives believing that we're in charge, that we made this or that thing happen, that the good things in our lives are a result of the effort we've put into them. On the other hand, when we assume a regular posture of prayer, we recognize that He is in charge, that He is at work in us, and that when we have good things in our life, they are always from our good Father. Prayer is a reminder of our position in life and in our relationships.

In Colossians 4:2, Paul urges the brethren there to continue steadfastly in prayer. This is not an occasional quick prayer when someone asks you to or when you're in trouble. This isn't praying at the dinner table and at church, then going on about your life. Instead, this is a continual conversation, a resolution to keep talking to God even when it gets difficult, even when you're frustrated, even when things are going great and it's far too easy to forget about your need for Him. He goes on to say that they should be watchful in prayer with thanksgiving. Being watchful here doesn't mean that if we don't pray about *sister so-and-so's* gall-bladder surgery, that it will escape God's notice and everything will go wrong. Instead, being watchful reminds us that we need to be in prayer. It won't escape God's notice, but if prayer escapes our notice, we will start having problems.

Finally, again, Paul pairs prayer with thanksgiving. Over and over those two concepts are linked, and with good reason. Sometimes we get stuck in thinking of prayer as a combination of a grocery list and a Santa list. We keep a list of everything we need to ask him for—sister so-and-so's gall-bladder surgery, safe travels for whomever—and expect to plop down on His lap, present our list, and have our wishes granted, as when the child goes to visit Santa. Of course, when we put it like that, it's obviously not the way prayer is supposed to work. Thanksgiving is the solution to our problem. I love teaching preschoolers in Bible class, not least because I love listening to them pray. You can actually hear them looking around the room—*"Thank you God for the Bible … and the paper … and the crayons … and the stapler …"* It's so refreshing to listen to the genuinely thankful tone of a child's prayer!

After exhorting the Colossians to be steadfast, watchful, and thankful in their prayers, Paul introduces a specific topic of prayer. In 4:3-4, he specifically asks them to pray for him. Of course, Paul is in prison. Any number of reasons to pray for Paul in prison present themselves. We should pray for his safety, for his health. We should pray for his release. We should pray for the Romans to be put down, since they're so obviously abusing their power in mistreating an innocent, godly man. But none of that is what Paul asks for. Paul instead asks the Colossians to pray for opportunities for Paul to preach. On top of that, when God provides those opportunities, Paul asks the Colossians to pray that he'll do a good job and teach clearly.

Whew! Paul had plenty to ask the Colossians to pray about. He was imprisoned, had some sort of thorn in the flesh that would have caused him physical difficulties, and was unjustly punished and persecuted. God had released prisoners before in the first-century church. Paul could have asked the Colossians to beg God for his release! He would be so much more useful out roaming around, teaching the gospel to everyone! However, Paul doesn't ask for deliverance from his ordeals. Instead, he asks the Colossians to pray that he'll bear up under them and continue to be useful to the church wherever he is.

In Colossians 4:5, Paul turns to a discussion of their walk. This may sound familiar. That's because it is. This is the same subject Paul's been on for most of the book. This is how Christ changes the way you behave, this time toward those who are outsiders. Specifically, he says to walk in wisdom toward outsiders. He also says to make the most of the time. So, what does that mean? A lot of things.

Sometimes we wish the Bible would tell us specifically how to handle those who aren't a part of God's church. How do I know who to be gentle with, and who just needs to be told the truth bluntly? How do I know whether to keep investing effort into this person, or if I should just wash my hands of them and call it done? If the Bible included a handy chart in the back— *"How to Know How to Handle Outsiders"*– that would make some things a lot easier. That's not what Paul offers, here, though. Instead, he says that knowing how to handle outsiders takes wisdom. There's not an easy, *one-size-fits-all* solution. Developing wisdom in this area, like all others, takes time and help. Pay attention to your interactions with people. Ask other, older kingdom workers how you ought to handle this or that situation. Most of all, heed the advice of James and ask God for wisdom, because He'll give it to you!

Part of Paul's admonition, though, also involves making the most of the time. This is such an important part of the wisdom of handling outsiders. It's tempting to think that we've got all the time in the world. *"Maybe I'll mention Jesus to the other soccer mom next time. Or next season. Maybe I'll work Jesus into the conversation with my family member next year at the holidays."* Or, just as often, maybe, *"If I browbeat my friend again about coming to church, it'll work this time."* A huge part of walking with wisdom toward outsiders is timing. Sometimes the time to speak is now. Sometimes the time to speak is not now. How can you possibly know the difference? Wisdom. Sorry, no easy answers here.

Finally here, Paul addresses their speech as it relates to outsiders. He's already talked about speech a lot elsewhere in the book. Here, though, he wants to talk specifically about how Christians ought to speak when it comes to those who haven't obeyed the gospel. He says that speech ought always to be gracious. This is speech that benefits the hearer, that gives gifts to the hearer, that makes the hearer better for having heard. Of course, this can be difficult when the hearer is an enemy of the gospel. Why should I speak in such a way that an enemy of the gospel is better for having heard me speak? The answer is in the first couple of chapters of Colossians. God has given us such great gifts, shown us such grace, and made us better to the point of being made into beings like His Son. How then do we speak graciously? By speaking the truth that God has spoken into our lives.

Paul compares this gracious speech to a dish being seasoned with salt. I have been known to undersalt my mashed potatoes. The result is not appetizing, to say the least. They're bland, uninspiring, and frankly not worth eating. So, with this history, I will also sometimes go overboard with the salt in my mashed potatoes. Friend, that's no better. While the potatoes are no longer bland, they're still not worth eating! As with mashed potatoes, our speech toward outsiders needs to strike just the right balance. Not too bland, but not too much either. How do we find that balance? You guessed it—wisdom.

Paul finishes this thought by saying that when speech is gracious, we will know how to answer each person. This is really a summary of the two verses here. When our speech is gracious, when we act with wisdom toward those who are outside, when we make the most of the time, we will know how to answer each person. We will learn who needs what reaction, who needs to hear what when. We will gain that wisdom that Paul urges.

Thought Questions

1. Where in your life is your biggest temptation to think you're in charge? How can prayer help with that?

2. What would need to change in your prayer life for it to become steadfast, watchful, and thankful?

3. What do we pray for most when we pray for others? Do we pray for physical deliverance or spiritual strength? What does Paul ask for here?

4. What trial are you enduring now that you should pray for strength through rather than deliverance from?

5. What are some tough situations you've seen in how to handle outsiders? Maybe your sisters in Christ have ideas on how to handle those!

6. Can you think of a time when timing affected the way you handled an outsider? How can that change the way you deal with outsiders in the future?

7. When has someone spoken graciously to you? How did it feel? How can you share this wonderful gift with others?

8. What outsiders are in your life? How can you change your behavior with them to be wise, timely, and gracious?

Paul's Friends
Colossians 4:7-18

Lesson 12: Paul's Friends

Now we come to the part of Colossians that no one ever studies! I don't think I've ever been in a class where we covered the greetings section of Colossians. There are probably two reasons for that. First, it's really hard to stick to the pacing of a lesson book, so most Bible classes I've been in don't finish the book. Second, though, this section seems difficult for us to connect with. Paul is sending greetings to and from a bunch of people we don't know and talking about some other people we don't know.

Nonetheless, there are several lessons to learn from this section. One of the biggest lessons overall in this section is the importance of connection. Paul has this section in most of his epistles, in which he talks to and about specific Christians he knows. Why on earth did the Holy Spirit think it relevant and appropriate to preserve these sections for us? It shows the importance of connection. Paul wasn't just writing these letters to pass on important doctrinal lessons for the churches to which he wrote. He wrote these letters because he dearly loved the people involved in the letters! If we consider Colossians as just a treatise on the doctrine involved, as opposed to considering it as a letter from Paul to some people he loved without even having met them, that changes the whole tone of the book.

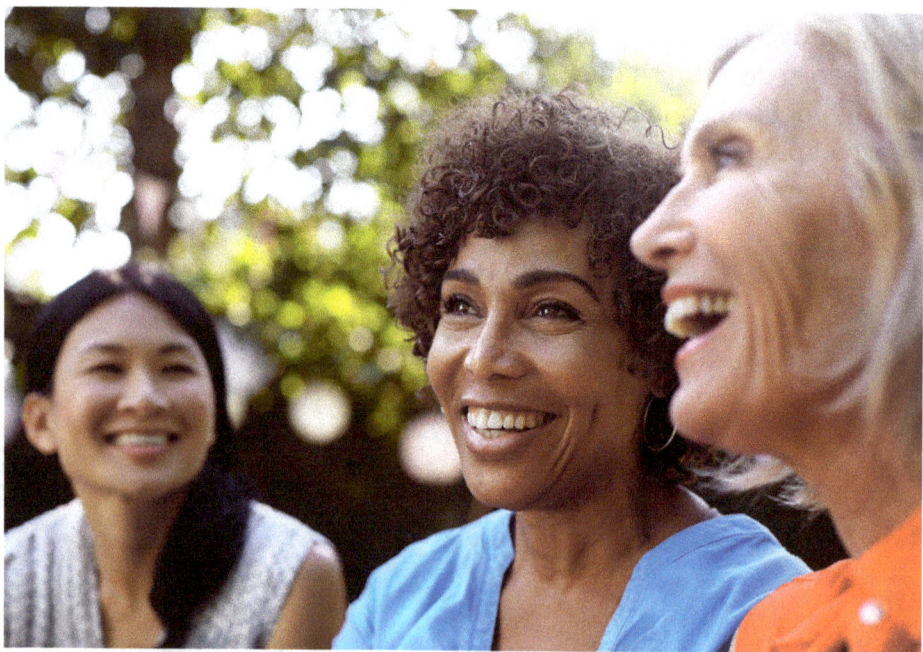

This section of the book also makes all of this real. It's easy to think of Paul as someone who is very one-dimensional. He's an apostle who marches along always doing the right thing and preaching doctrine steadfastly without feelings or emotions or relationships. Of course, that's not the case! Paul's greetings sections remind us that he's a real person with real feelings. The greetings section in 2 Timothy 4 shows that clearly—"Demas has abandoned me; only Luke is left." Sections like

these flesh out the realness of the people of the Bible and remind us that it's okay for us to have feelings and relationships, too!

Some of the names in Paul's greetings section in Colossians are familiar. Luke appears toward the end of the section, and we know him as a frequent companion of Paul's on his journeys. We see the constancy of some of Paul's companions in stories like Luke's. Demas is mentioned in this letter as being with Paul and greeting the church. Demas's inclusion reminds us that people change. Some people are like Luke, constant and faithful. Others are like Demas, companions for a time who are then called away by worldly concerns.

Paul tells them that Tychicus and Onesimus are headed to see them as well. It sounds like Tychicus isn't as well known to the Colossians, but Onesimus is one of their own. Paul is sending them to reassure the Colossians of Paul's well-being and to update them on all that is going on where Paul is. Part of the lesson we can take from this mention of these two men is the importance of connection. Paul has people around him who are also dear to those to whom he is writing. He writes to the Colossians about doctrine and how they ought to live, but this last section is all about people. Paul cares about the Colossians enough that he wants them to be updated on how everything is going with him.

Do we have connections with Christians in other places? Is it important to us when someone arrives from another part of the country or the world to find out how the church fares in that area? The Colossians were hungry enough for that information that Paul reassured them here at the end of the letter that he was sending two separate people to feed that desire for connection. We should be encouraged when we meet Christians from other places by news of how the spread of the gospel goes in those locations.

Paul mentions three men who are the only Jewish Christians with him at this point: Aristarchus, Barnabas's cousin Mark, and Justus. Aristarchus is apparently also a prisoner for the sake of the gospel. Mark is known enough to the Colossians that Paul has told them that they should welcome him if he shows up in Colossae. Justus doesn't really have any notes with his inclusion, just his name. These three men greet the Christians in Colossae—though they aren't mentioned as being well acquainted with the church there, they are connected to them anyway, through Jesus.

Epaphras gets his second mention in the book, and Paul tells them a number of things about the work that Epaphras has been doing. He

Ruins of Ancient Laodicea

mentions that Epaphras is doing a good job where he is, setting to ease any worries that the Colossians might have about him representing the home folks well. We also see the maturity of Epaphras, that he works constantly in prayer for the Colossians, that they might mature. Epaphras is on board with Paul's message and mission, and he prays that the Colossians will continue to mature and bear fruit for Jesus.

Paul also has a few greetings of his own to pass on to nearby churches. He mentions the church in Laodicea specifically, and says for the Colossian brethren to greet the Laodicean brethren. Paul mentions having written a letter to Laodicea and wants the Colossians and Laodiceans to exchange letters at some point. While the Bible obviously hasn't preserved the Laodicean letter *(unless it's Philemon)*, it's important for us to realize that the Bible books we have aren't the only letters ever written, even by inspired writers. Paul cared as much for the church in Laodicea as he did for the church in Colossae, even though we only have one of those letters.

His final instruction is an interesting one: he sends a very specific message to a Christian named Archippus. He wants the Colossian brethren to remind Archippus, when they see him, to do what Paul told him to and fulfill the ministry God has given him. We don't know much about this instruction. We don't know whether Archippus was resisting

the ministry God had given him, and he needed to be rebuked for so doing, or if Archippus was trying, and he needed encouragement from the brethren. What we know, however, is that Paul tasked the Colossians with reminding Archippus what needed to be done. Similarly, we need to be on the lookout in our lives for the people that need a little extra push to keep doing the work God has for them. Whether it's the preacher who needs encouragement or the sister who's resisting teaching Bible classes, we should be watching for opportunities to help people fulfill God's ministry in their lives. We also need to be open to reminders from others in our lives when people see ministries in our lives that we're neglecting.

God intends for this walk as Christians to be a companionable one. We are not meant to walk through life alone, trying our best on our own to honor the agreement we've made with God. We need each other! Sometimes we need each other to be encouraging. Sometimes we need each other to be the fire underneath us. Sometimes we just need to know that others are doing the same kind of things we're doing! Regardless of what the specific need is, God created the church to be a place for us to find companionship.

Thought Questions

1. How does connection with someone change how you communicate with them? Why is that important?

2. For each of the people below, mentioned in this section, make notes about who they are and what Paul says about them. Do you have a person like this in your life? Who?

Luke

Demas

Tychicus

Onesimus

Aristarchus

Mark

Epaphras

The Laodiceans

Archippus

3. How can you walk with other Christians in your life this week?

Review

Lesson 13: Review

It's easy to get bogged down in the details of a book like Colossians. There's a lot in the book, and it's some meaty writing! The details are important, too—there is important doctrinal truth contained in the epistle. If we only look for specific doctrinal teaching, though, we stand a chance of missing equally important themes in the book.

Paul's central theme in the book of Colossians is the preeminence of Jesus. Those of us who have been Christians for decades might be tempted to *handwave* that—*"yes, yes, we know, Jesus is super important."* In this epistle, though, Paul encourages us to get past that handwaving and really sit down and think about just how important and crucial and absolutely awe-inspiring Jesus truly is. Yes, He is the Son of God, but there's more. Yes, He is the Savior of mankind, but there's more. Yes, He is the example for all of us, but there's more! No matter what you think you know about Jesus and His *amazingness*, there's always more. He is more than we can wrap our heads around.

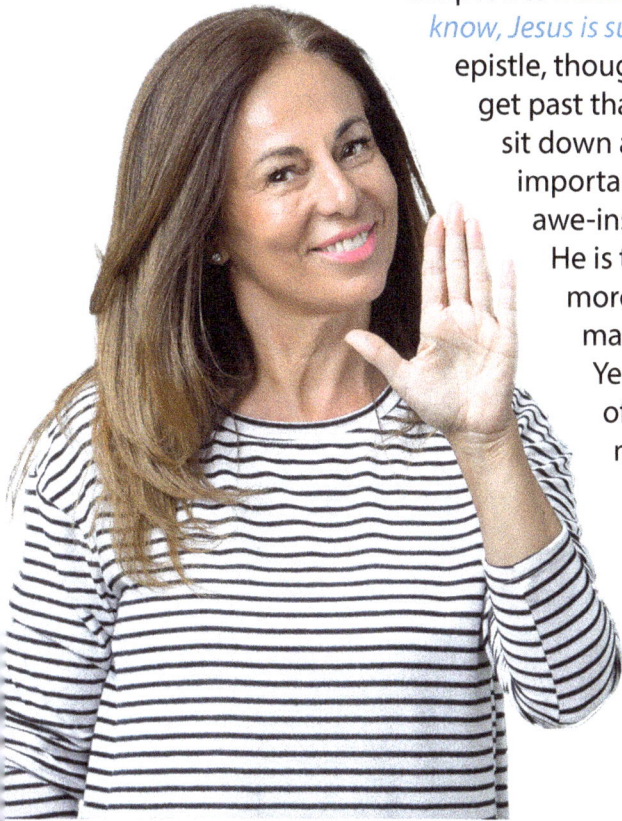

He doesn't stop there, though. Paul spends the rest of the book explaining how Jesus's preeminence changes us. Recognizing that preeminence is only the first step of the process. The rest of the process is translating that recognition into change. Jesus should prompt you to change how you think about yourself and your worth. Jesus should prompt you to change how you think about the worth of those around you. Jesus should push you to change your relationships with people around you and the things that you value and pursue. Jesus should change everything about your life!

All of these instructions aren't standalone teachings. They aren't meant to be learned in a vacuum. They're all connected with each other. The changes in your life don't happen on their own; they happen because of Jesus. Jesus's *awesomeness* isn't just something that you observe and acknowledge; it's something that you let sink into you until it changes you at the very core of who you are.

To review our study of the book of Colossians, use the space below to outline the book. Use colors or symbols to connect related ideas as you find them throughout the book. Be prepared to talk through the outline you've made! Use the following questions to help guide your outlining and connection.

Outline of the Book

Thought Questions

1. What themes in Paul's prayers show up elsewhere in the letter?

2. Where does Paul reference back to Jesus being the best of everything?

3. How does reconciliation through Jesus play into the applications made later in the book?

4. What aspects of Paul's struggles become relevant to other sections of the book?

5. What traditions and philosophies are evident throughout the book as having taken the Colossians captive?

6. How does not passing judgment about traditions show up elsewhere in the letter?

7. Why are the things above the ones the Colossians should seek, based on the first part of the book?

8. How are peace and submission related to the discussion of Jesus's preeminence early in the letter?

www.ingramcontent.com/pod-product-compliance
Lightning Source LLC
Chambersburg PA
CBHW051431090426
42737CB00014B/2914